Outstanding Dissertations in

ECONOMICS

A Continuing Garland Research Series

Investment and the Value of Capital

Andrew B. Abel

Garland Publishing, Inc.
New York & London, 1979

Library of Congress Cataloging in Publication Data

Abel, Andrew B 1952–
Investment and the value of capital.

(Outstanding dissertations in economics)
Originally presented as the author's thesis, Massachusetts Institute of Technology, 1978.
Bibliography: p.
1. Capital investments—Mathematical models. 2. Capital investments—United States—Mathematical models. I. Title. II. Series.
HG4028.C4A217 1979 332′.0415 78–75063
ISBN 0–8240–4139–9

All volumes in this series are printed on acid-free, 250-year-life paper.

Printed in the United States of America.

INVESTMENT AND THE VALUE OF CAPITAL

By

ANDREW BRUCE ABEL

A.B., Princeton University

(1974)

Submitted in Partial Fulfillment
Of the Requirements For The
Degree of

DOCTOR OF PHILOSOPHY

At The

MASSACHUSETTS INSTITUTE OF TECHNOLOGY

May 1978

Signature of Author...
Department of Economics, May 11, 1978

Certified by...
Thesis Supervisor

Accepted by...
Chairman, Department Committee

INVESTMENT AND THE VALUE OF CAPITAL

By

Andrew Bruce Abel

Submitted to the Department of Economics
on May 11, 1978 in partial fulfillment of the requirements
for the Degree of Doctor of Philosophy.

ABSTRACT

This dissertation develops a variant of the market value approach to the determination of investment. Investment in capital is shown to be an increasing function of the shadow price of installed capital relative to the cost of investment. This model of investment behavior is the unifying feature of the four essays in this dissertation.

The first essay of this dissertation integrates the conventional neoclassical model of investment with the investment model based on the shadow price of capital. The shadow price model allows for a much richer analysis of dynamics and is used to study the dynamic responses to exogenous shocks. The tax policy analysis of the neoclassical model is adapted to the framework of the shadow price model and permits us to study the effects of certain fiscal policies of varying durations. This essay also demonstrates that the relative pattern of dynamic responses to shocks that has been attributed to putty-clay models can also be derived within a putty-putty framework.

The second essay is an attempt to empirically estimate an investment equation based on the shadow price of capital. This model depends greatly on expectations about future rentals to capital. In order to deal with the problem of expectations and revisions in expectations, a new estimation technique based on distributed leads is developed. Although the technique could use much refinement, it appears to work rather well.

The third essay is addressed to the current policy issue of how to stimulate investment. The policy tools compared are an investment tax credit and a corporate tax cut. We find that for permanent policy changes, the investment tax credit can achieve a given stimulus to investment at a smaller cost to the Treasury than can a corporate tax cut. However, the relative costs of equivalent temporary fiscal policies are ambiguous, although there is a presumption that the investment tax credit is cheaper in this case also.

The final essay examines the implications of limited *ex post* substitutability for investment behavior and capacity utilization. In a standard putty-putty model without limited *ex post* substitutability, it is never optimal for a cost minimizing firm to have idle capital. This essay treats labor as a quasi-fixed factor of production to achieve limited *ex post* substitutability. Within this framework there can be optimal variations in capacity utilization. We find that in the absence of shocks to the system, capacity utilization and investment in fixed capital are negatively related, contrary to the conventional presumption. However, in response to unanticipated shocks, investment and capacity do move in the same direction. This essay also examines tax policy within the framework of limited *ex post* substitutability.

Thesis Supervisor: Rudiger Dornbusch
Associate Professor of Economics

ACKNOWLEDGMENTS

Perhaps the most difficult part of writing a dissertation is selecting a set of related interesting questions and formulating an approach to analyze them. I owe a tremendous thanks to Rudi Dornbusch for helping me select the area of investment and for guiding my research on this topic. Over the last year and a half, Rudi provided me with countless comments, suggestions, and criticisms. He listened to all my ideas with great patience and showed an uncanny ability to sort out the good ideas from the not-so-good ideas. The essays in this dissertation clearly bear the mark of Rudi's influence and I am grateful for it. Although Rudi was my principal advisor, I received excellent advice from Stan Fischer and Jerry Hausman. Both Stan and Jerry provided me with concise and insightful criticisms on my work. My intellectual debt to each of them extends back beyond my dissertation to my first year of graduate school. In three semesters of statistics and econometrics, Jerry taught me virtually all that I know in these fields. As for monetary theory and macroeconomics, it was Stan who first cultivated my interest in, and understanding of, these fields. Hopefully, I brought together some elements from all these fields in writing this dissertation.

One benefit of the graduate program at M.I.T. is that thoughtful comments from excellent economists are readily available either through workshops or informal discussions. Among those faculty and students whose comments contributed to this dissertation are Pedro Aspe, Olivier Blanchard, Paul Krugman, Franco Modigliani, Tom Rothenberg, Robert Solow, and especially Dick Startz, with whom I discussed my ideas almost every morning over coffee. The National Science Foundation and the Federal Reserve Bank of Boston provided financial assistance. I greatly appreciate the assistance of all those people who helped me complete this dissertation. They are not responsible for any errors that remain.

I would like to thank my parents for giving me the luxury of obtaining the best education available without having to worry about its cost. They have been a constant source of encouragement throughout my 21 years of formal education. Finally, I would like to thank my fiancee, Anne, for her patience, understanding, and encouragement in the face of the many ups and downs of this dissertation. In so many ways, she made the past year truly wonderful.

TABLE OF CONTENTS

TABLE OF CONTENTS (Continued)

TABLE OF CONTENTS (Continued)

Introduction

This dissertation is a collection of four essays on investment. To place these essays in context, it is helpful to review briefly the development of the investment literature. This review makes no pretense of being complete; rather, it is a brief summary of the highlights of investment theory that are relevant to this dissertation.

As with most of macroeconomics, the natural starting point for a brief review of the development of investment is the General Theory. In Chapter 11, Keynes defines the marginal efficiency of capital to be the discount rate for which the present value of the costs associated with a new unit of capital is equal to the present value of the revenues accruing to that unit. He then argues that the marginal efficiency of capital is a decreasing function of the rate of investment, and in any period of time,the rate of investment is such as to make the marginal efficiency of capital equal to the interest rate. Since the marginal efficiency of capital is a decreasing function of the rate of investment, the rate of investment is a decreasing function of the interest rate. This Keynesian investment equation has often been misrepresented in textbook expositions. It is generally asserted that the marginal efficiency of capital is a decreasing function of the rate of investment because the marginal product of capital is a decreasing function of the size of the capital stock, and higher rates of investment make larger additions to the capital stock. While it is true that the marginal product of capital is a decreasing function of the stock of capital, variations in the rate of investment do not significantly affect the size of the capital stock for short intervals of time. Keynes recognized this point (p. 136) and argued instead that the marginal efficiency of capital is a decreasing function of the rate of investment because of the rising flow supply price of capital goods. A high rate of investment requires a high supply price of new capital goods, and the present value of the revenues accruing to capital will be equal to this high supply price only if the discount rate is sufficiently low. Thus, it is the rising supply curve of new capital goods which makes the schedule of marginal efficiency of capital slope downward as a function of the rate of investment, for short intervals of time. Since the marginal efficiency of capital is set equal to the interest rate, investment is a decreasing function of the interest rate.

Since capital is durable, the marginal efficiency of capital depends on the expectations of future returns as well as the current return to capital. In order to get a measure of the expectations of future rentals to capital, Keynes turns to asset markets in Chapter 12. The stock market assigns the proper value to the stream of returns accruing to a unit of capital. The rate of investment is an increasing function of the market value of newly installed capital goods as suggested by the following often-quoted passage:

> "But the daily revaluations of the Stock Exchange, though they are primarily made to facilitate transfers of old investments between one individual and another, inevitably exert a decisive influence on the rate of current investment. For there is no sense in building up a new enterprise at a cost greater than that at which a similar existing enterprise can be purchased; whilst there is an inducement to spend on a new project what may seem an extravagant sum, if it can be floated off on the Stock Exchange at an immediate profit."
>
> (p. 151)

We shall refer to the approach in Chapter 11 as the "structural approach" since it requires firms to examine the stream of returns to capital over the entire life of the capital. The approach of Chapter 12 will be called the "market value approach". These two approaches are essentially the same; they differ only in emphasis. The structural approach looks behind the market value of capital to the determinants of market value. The distinction is drawn here because the literature has followed two separate streams.

The market value approach has been popularized by Tobin (1961, 1969). Tobin defines the variable q to be the ratio of the market value of installed capital to the replacement cost of capital. In the spirit of the passage from Keynes cited above, Tobin argues that investment is an increasing function of q. Although Tobin's work has been theoretical, one of his students, Ciccolo (1975), estimated an investment equation based on q. Recently, other works which examine the empirical relationship between investment and the market value of capital have appeared, including Engle and Foley (1975) and the Economic Report of the President (1977).

Within the structural approach to investment, we distinguish between the empirical branch and the theoretical branch. The empirical work on structural investment equations was pioneered by Jorgenson and collaborators. In principle, Jorgenson recognized the durability of capital and the role of expectations implied by this durability. However, in practice, a very static expectations mechanism is used to derive the demand for capital goods. This approach derives a stock demand for capital goods. Investment is then determined by means of an apparently *ad hoc* stock adjustment mechanism, in which investment is an increasing function of the gap between the desired stock of capital, K*, and the current existing stock of capital, K_t. This approach ignores the role of the rising supply curve of new capital goods in determining the rate of investment.

Although the empirical structural approach has many weaknesses, it has flourished over the last decade and a half. Because this model is structural, it provides a useful framework for policy analysis. Hall and Jorgenson (1967, 1969, 1971) have used this model to examine the effects on investment of the corporate tax rate, the depreciation allowance, and the investment tax credit. The original Jorgenson model has undergone some refinements, the most notable of which is the inclusion of the putty-clay hypothesis. Under the putty-clay hypothesis, installed capital is assumed to be less malleable than uninstalled capital, so that the *ex post* elasticity of substitution between labor and capital is smaller than the corresponding *ex ante* elasticity. Bischoff (1971) developed the implications of this assumption and demonstrated that investment responds more rapidly to an increase in expected output than to an equivalent decrease in the cost of capital.

The theoretical branch of the structural approach to investment developed at about the same time as the empirical branch. This work was developed by Eisner and Strotz (1963), Lucas (1967a), Gould (1968), and Treadway (1969). Their work recognized the role of expectations that is implied by the durability of capital. However, rather than treating the future as uncertain they assumed that firms had perfect foresight and based their decisions on explicit intertemporal optimization.

This treatment of expectations is the polar opposite case of the static expectations used by the empirical structural branch. Each branch of the structural approach is forced to make some simplifying assumption about expectations. Indeed, it is the treatment of expectations which is the major weakness of the structural approach. Note that the market value approach is free from this problem since it relies on well-functioning asset markets to make forecasts and properly digest expectations. However, in avoiding the expectations problem, the market value approach loses the ability to examine the effects of policy on investment through a structural model.

The theoretical structural approach derives a determinate rate of investment by appealing to a rising flow supply curve of investment goods. The rising supply curve is achieved formally by assuming that there is an adjustment cost function which is an increasing convex function of the rate of investment. It was shown by Eisner and Strotz, Lucas, Gould and Treadway that the rate of investment derived from the optimizing behavior of firms facing convex adjustment costs may be represented as a flexible accelerator. That is, investment is proportional to the gap between K^* and K_t. This derivation of the flexible accelerator from optimizing behavior provided a partial justification for the stock adjustment formulation used by Jorgenson and others. However, the justification for the stock adjustment mechanism was not unqualified. The speed of adjustment was shown to depend on other parameters of the system. For example, in the Gould model, the gap between K^* and K_t closes at a rate equal to the rate of physical depreciation. Since the empirical structural approach takes K^*, K_t and the physical depreciation rate as exogenous, there would be nothing left to be estimated in an investment equation derived from the Gould model, with static expectations.

It is interesting to note the influence of a major development in optimization theory on the development of investment theory. The dynamic optimization problem of the firm was solved by Lucas and Gould as a standard calculus of variations problem using Euler's method. This solution method yields a second-order differential equation in the capital stock. This second-order equation is attacked by defining an auxiliary variable and rewriting the second-order equation as a two-equation system of first-order differential equations. In light of the maximum principle of Pontryagin, we recognize the auxiliary variable as a function of the shadow price of capital. However, these papers were written before Pontryagin's maximum principle had found its way into economics, so that this interpretation is not given to the auxiliary variable. Arrow (1968) solves the firm's dynamic optimization problem using the maximum principle and the shadow price of capital. However, he does not point out that investment is an increasing function of the shadow price of capital. Mussa (1974, 1977) observes that investment is an increasing function of the shadow price of installed capital and notes the link to Tobin's q approach. The difference is that dynamic optimiza- yields investment as a function of the shadow price of installed capital, whereas Tobin's q depends on the market price.

The theoretical structural works discussed above all assumed that there were increasing marginal costs of adjustment at the level of the individual firm. Others, such as Witte (1963) and Foley and Sidrauski

(1970), have assumed that for individual firms, the flow supply curve of capital goods is horizontal, but the supply curve for the economy as a whole is upward sloping. These models also yield the rate of investment as an increasing function of the price of capital goods.

Against this background of the development of investment, we can examine the contribution of this dissertation. Essay I, "Investment Theory: An Integration of Two Approaches," is an attempt to link the empirical structural approach of Jorgenson with the market value approach of Tobin. These two approaches are linked via the theoretical structural approach. More specifically, we first develop the connection between Jorgenson's model and the theoretical structural model. The important difference between the empirical and theoretical branches of the structural approach is that the theoretical branch relies on an upward sloping flow supply curve of new capital goods to determine the rate of investment. However, the empirical work of Jorgenson, with its stock adjustment mechanism, depends on some immutable structure of delivery lags to determine the rate of investment. Therefore, it is difficult to see how these two approaches can be completely reconciled. However, in steady state equilibrium, it is shown that these two versions of the structural approach are equivalent. The theoretical structural approach is the same as Tobin's q approach if we identify the shadow price of installed capital with the market price. Thus the theoretical structural approach, which incorporates explicit intertemporal optimization, provides the link between the approaches of Jorgenson and Tobin. After reconciling these two models of investment behavior, Essay I borrows the tax policy analysis from Hall and Jorgenson and embeds it into the theoretical structural model. This framework is especially convenient for analyzing the dynamic responses to policy, whether anticipated or unanticipated. The analysis of anticipated exogenous policy shocks allows us to examine the dynamic responses to a temporary investment tax credit. Finally, Essay I demonstrates that the so-called putty-clay response patterns to exogenous shocks, as discussed by Bischoff, can be derived from a putty-putty model.

Essay II, "Investment, q, and Rational Expectations," estimates an investment equation derived from the theoretical structural model. This paper aims to escape from two of the serious pitfalls contained in most of the existing empirical work on investment equations. First, this paper avoids reliance on estimated polynomial distributed lags in the belief that this technique has too large an element of "curve fitting". Second, this paper replaces the static expectations mechanism implicit in much of the empirical structural work with rational expectations. The specification of an equation which depends on the rational expectation of the present value of a stream of future returns is a difficult problem. We manage to handle this problem by deriving a Koyck lead specification and paying attention to revisions in expectations. The results of estimating this investment equation, in which the shadow price of capital is an explanatory variable, are in line with Ciccolo's estimates based on q. We readily admit that the estimation technique of this paper leaves much room for improvement. Such improvement would seem to be a worthwhile endeavor since this estimation technique could be applied to equations dealing with any type of durable good. An obvious application of this estimation procedure is to the permanent income consumption function. Consumption depends on wealth, i.e., the present value of the stream of income accruing to an individual, just as investment depends on the present value of the stream of returns to a unit of capital. Hence, the specification and estimation procedure for a consumption function would be similar to that for an investment equation.

Essay III, "Fiscal Stimulus to Investment: Tax Cut or Investment Tax Credit?" analyzes a current policy question within the theoretical structural framework developed in Essay I. Equivalent fiscal policies are defined as those policies having the same effect on the rate of investment. This essay compares the tax revenues to the Treasury under alternative policies and concludes that a permanent investment tax credit is cheaper to the Treasury than an equivalent permanent corporate tax cut. There is a presumption that this result is also valid for explicitly temporary policies. The barrier to strong results for the temporary case is that the results are sensitive to the time pattern of the depreciation allowance. Although Essay III is directed toward an interesting policy question, it also provides a convenient framework for a few methodological comments on the flexible accelerator.

Essay IV, "Limited *Ex Post* Substitutability and Optimal Variations in Capacity Utilization," examines investment behavior in a model in which the *ex post* elasticity of substitution of labor for capital is less than the *ex ante* elasticity of substitution. This analysis was motivated by criticism of putty-putty models, i.e., models in which existing capital is assumed to be as malleable, *ex post*, as is future uninstalled capital, *ex ante*. In a putty-putty model with costlessly adjustable labor, a cost minimizing firm will never have idle capital. However, this essay uses limited *ex post* substitutability of labor and capital, combined with labor adjustment costs, to develop an optimizing model in which there are variations in capacity utilization. Even in this putty-clay type model, investment is driven by the shadow price of installed capital. This model produces the unconventional result that capacity utilization and investment in fixed capital are negatively related over time, in the absence of shocks. However, in response to unanticipated demand shocks, capacity utilization and investment move in the same direction.

The four essays in this dissertation employ a common framework to study issues in investment theory. Although this framework has been very fruitful, it does suffer from certain shortcomings. The models used throughout this dissertation are partial equilibrium in nature. Wages, output prices, and the discount rate are assumed to be exogenous. If this model is to be used to explain aggregate investment, then presumably investment has a multiplier effect on output. However, this endogeneity of output demand has been ignored. Another problem is that the theoretical analysis has assumed perfect foresight on the part of firms. Perfect foresight is a convenient approximation, but we must recognize that uncertainty can affect market value and firm behavior. Uncertainty and considerations of diversification in the spirit of the capital asset pricing model would cause the shadow price of capital, as calculated in these essays, to differ from the market value of capital. Despite these shortcomings, however, the four essays in this dissertation seem to tie together some strands of the literature and to fill certain gaps.

ESSAY I

INVESTMENT THEORY: AN INTEGRATION OF TWO APPROACHES

I. Introduction

The literature on investment theory in the last decade and a half has been divided into two streams of thought: the standard neoclassical (SNC) approach[1] developed by Jorgenson and others, and the q approach developed by Tobin. This paper attempts to integrate the two approaches and to explicitly take account of adjustment costs. The SNC approach treats the flow of investment as a response to desired changes in the stock of capital. Jorgenson derives an expression for the optimal level of capital within a Cobb-Douglas framework given the level of output, the price of output, the cost of capital, and the elasticity of output with respect to capital. Net investment is then an incremental flow of capital goods to (partially) close the gap between the desired and the actual stock of capital. A major criticism of this approach is that there is no mechanism determining the _rate_ of investment. The rate of investment is determined in an _ad hoc_ manner by treating current investment as a distributed lag response to current and previous desired changes in the stock of capital. The partial adjustment process associated with the distributed lag is due to a fixed structure of delivery lags, which is the same for large changes in the stock of capital as for small changes in the stock of capital.

In Tobin's approach, the crucial variable determining the flow of investment is q, the ratio of the market value of new capital goods to their replacement cost. If the market values new capital

---

[1] I follow the lead of Bischoff (1971) in referring to this approach as the standard neoclassical one.

goods highly relative to their replacement cost, i.e., if $q > 1$, then there will be an incentive for firms to invest. Firms buy output in the (one-sector) goods market and install the capital in place. The marginal installation cost, and hence the marginal cost of installed capital, is an increasing function of the rate of investment and firms will select a rate of investment at which the marginal cost is equal to q. Hence the rate of investment is an increasing function of q. This approach is also subject to the criticism that the rate of investment is determined in an *ad hoc* manner because the installation cost function is no less *ad hoc* than an assumed structure of delivery lags. However, in this essay we choose to rely on installation costs rather than on an immutable structure of delivery lags because the installation cost formulation allows firms to control the time path of the installation of a given increment of capital by changing the per unit installation cost they are willing to pay. That is, the speed with which a given increment of capital is installed is a function of economic factors in addition to technological constraints.

These two approaches also differ in their emphasis on the underlying determinants of investment. The SNC approach is basically a demand for capital goods (capital services are assumed proportional to the stock of capital) in which the demand for capital is derived from the underlying aggregate production function of the economy. Given the production function, output, and relative prices, there is a desired stock of capital and hence a demand for a change in the size of the capital stock. The rate of investment is driven by a quantity signal. On the other hand, the q approach places the aggregate production function in the background. The stock market values new capital and hence determines q. Clearly, some notion of the underlying production function, as well as factor prices and future output, is involved in the stock market's valuation of capital, although this is not chosen as the focal point in Tobin's analysis. The important point to note is that q, a relative price determined by the market, drives investment. In Tobin's approach, it is a price signal, rather than a quantity signal which drives investment.

In this essay we develop a partial equilibrium model of investment using elements of both approaches. We follow the spirit of the SNC approach in working with an aggregate Cobb-Douglas production function, given relative prices and output. However, the rate of investment is determined by equating the marginal cost of newly installed capital with its marginal value, rather than relying on fixed delivery lags. The results obtained using this modified q-approach are consistent with the SNC approach.

Section II derives an expression for q under the myopic assumption that firms ignore future net investment when making current investment decisions. This simple analysis allows us to examine clearly many implications of the model. However, the dynamics of the system with myopic firms is not rich enough to provide answers to certain interesting questions, so we develop a more forward-looking analysis in Section III. Installation costs are discussed in Section IV and Section V solves a dynamic intertemporal optimization problem which explicitly incorporates adjustment costs. The results are shown to be the same as those derived in Section III. Section VI analyzes the effects of anticipated and unanticipated exogenous shocks, with special attention to the investment tax credit. In Section VII, we use the putty-putty model of this essay to reinterpret some implications of the putty-clay hypothesis and to challenge the empirical evidence supporting the putty-clay hypothesis. Concluding remarks are presented in Section VIII.

II. The Value of Installed Capital

A. Net Investment

In this subsection, we develop a very simple one-sector partial equilibrium model of the valuation of installed capital goods. We assume that the aggregate production function is Cobb-Douglas, so that $Q_s = AL_s^{\alpha}K_s^{1-\alpha}$, where Q_s is output, L_s is labor input, and K_s is the capital stock. In determining investment plans, starting today at time t, the representative firm takes as given the expected path of output Q_s, $s \geq t$.[1] In addition, the real wage rate is expected to remain at $\bar{w}$ forever, and future earnings are capitalized at rate r. Finally, in order to concentrate on net investment, we assume that depreciation is zero, so that gross investment equals net investment.

The marginal unit of installed capital should be valued at the present discounted value of the net cash flow which it creates. Ignoring depreciation and taxes, the net cash flow at time s attributable to the marginal unit of capital is equal to the reduction in the wage bill required to produce the output Q_s. Note that the wage bill saving is equal to

$$-\bar{w}\frac{dL_s}{dK_s}\bigg|_{Q_s = \text{constant}} ,$$

that is, the wage rate multiplied by the marginal rate of substitution of labor for capital. For the Cobb-Douglas production function assumed in this essay, the wage bill saving is equal to

---

[1] In this essay we examine the behavior of a cost-minimizing firm which takes the path of output as given. See Essays III and IV for investment behavior of firms which choose their output paths as well as their investment paths.

$$\bar{w}\,\frac{1-\alpha}{\alpha}\left(\frac{Q_s}{AK_s}\right)^{1/\alpha} .$$

Calculating the present discounted value of these wage bill savings over the life of an additional unit of capital installed at time t, we obtain an expression for V_t, the market value of an installed unit of capital

$$V_t = \int_t^{\infty} \frac{1-\alpha}{\alpha}\,\bar{w}\left(\frac{Q_s}{AK_s}\right)^{1/\alpha} e^{-r(s-t)}ds . \tag{II.A.1}$$

In this one-sector model, we let output be numeraire so that the price of uninstalled capital goods is equal to one. Therefore, the expression for V_t above also gives the value of q_t.

In order to evaluate the expression for q_t, we need to know the future path of output and the future path of the capital stock. We assume that output grows exponentially at rate g so that $Q_s = AL_tK_te^{g(s-t)}$, $s \geq t$. As for the path of the capital stock, we make the myopic assumption that the representative firm ignores its future net investment.[1] Therefore, $K_s = K_t$ for all $s \geq t$. Substituting for Q_s and K_s in (II.A.1) and recalling that $q_t = V_t$ we obtain[2]

---

[1]This is an unusual form of myopia in that there is perfect foresight with respect to output and wage rates but static expectations about the capital stock. In Section III, we correct this myopia.

[2]This expression is valid only if the integral in (II.A.1) is finite, i.e., only if the discount rate r exceeds g/α).

$$\text{(II.A.2)} \quad \text{a.} \quad q_t = \frac{1-\alpha}{\alpha} \bar{w} \left(\frac{Q_t}{AK_t} \right)^{1/\alpha} \frac{1}{r-g/\alpha}$$

$$\text{b.} \quad = \frac{1-\alpha}{\alpha} \bar{w} \frac{L_t}{K_t} \frac{1}{r-g/\alpha}$$

The expression for q_t above appears to be quite reasonable. Observe that an increase in the real wage rate $\bar{w}$ implies that a given reduction in labor input leads to an increased saving in the wage bill from an additional unit of capital. A lower rate of discount r implies that investors value future savings in wage costs more highly and hence value installed capital more highly. A higher rate of output growth g tends to increase the future demand for both inputs, labor and capital, and hence increases the incentive to invest. Finally, if the labor capital ratio (or the output capital ratio) is too high, there will be an incentive to reduce it through investment. All of the effects cited here tend to raise q at time t and hence tend to increase the rate of investment.

Connection with the SNC Approach

In order to illustrate the connection between the q approach and the SNC approach, we examine the market for capital services. We assume that the supply of capital services at any instant of time is proportional to the existing stock of installed capital, and hence the supply of capital services must be fixed at any point of time. Therefore, in Figure II.1 the supply curve of capital services is vertical. Along the demand curve for capital services, the rental rate c is equal to the wage bill saving accruing to the marginal unit of capital, $\frac{1-\alpha}{\alpha}\bar{w}\left(\frac{Q}{AK}\right)^{1/\alpha}$. Therefore,

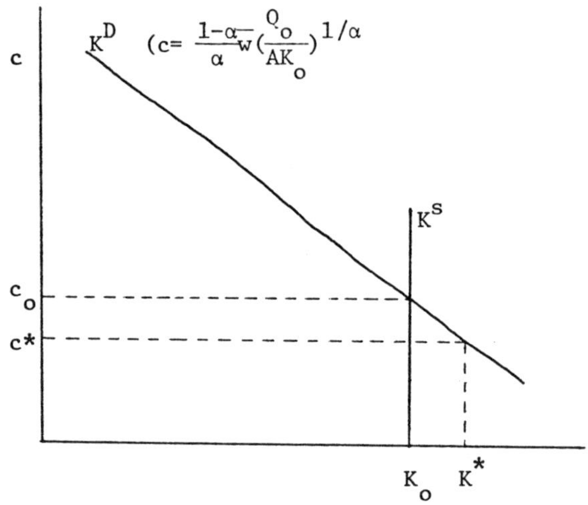

Figure II-1

the market-clearing rental price for capital services at time t is $c_t = \frac{1-\alpha}{\alpha}\bar{w}\left(\frac{Q_t}{AK_t}\right)^{1/\alpha}$ and the expression for V_t in (II.A.1) is simply the discounted value of equilibrium rentals accruing to the marginal unit of capital. To simplify the exposition, we assume that output is expected to remain constant forever, i.e., g = 0, so that from (II.A.2), $q_t = \frac{1-\alpha}{\alpha}\frac{wL_t}{rK_t}$. There will be positive investment as long as $q_t > 1$, that is, as long as $K_t < \frac{1-\alpha}{\alpha}\frac{wL_t}{r}$. But, as shown below, this is precisely the same criterion as for the SNC model in this simple framework.

In the SNC approach, the desired level of capital, K*, is equal to $\frac{(1-\alpha)Q}{c}$ where c is the rental price of capital services. The relevant value of c is not the market-clearing rental c_t, but rather the long-run value c^*.[1] In the absence of depreciation, and with $\dot{q} = 0$ in the long run, $c^* = rq^*$, where q^* is the long-run price of capital goods. In this one-sector model with output as numeraire, $q^* = 1$, so that $c^* = r$. Therefore, the desired value of the capital stock is $K^* = \frac{(1-\alpha)Q}{r} = \frac{1-\alpha}{\alpha}\frac{wL}{r}$ and there will be net investment if $K_t < K^*$. This is the same criterion for investment as in the q approach above. In this simple model, without depreciation, both approaches lead to the same long-run capital stock.[2]

B. Replacement Investment

In the last subsection it was not necessary to distinguish between gross investment and net investment because, in the absence of depreciation, they are identical. We now wish to consider replacement investment, which is equal to gross investment less net investment, i.e., depreciation. In order to focus our attention on replacement investment, we examine a situation in which steady state net investment is zero. In keeping with our partial equilibrium framework we continue to assume a fixed wage rate $\bar{w}$ and a fixed discount rate r. The capital stock depreciates at a constant exponential rate δ. We also assume

---

[1] If the relevant value of c were the market-clearing value c_t, then K^* would be equal to K_t and there would be no net investment.

[2] If there were physical depreciation, this analysis would be slightly more cumbersome since in the q approach, q would exceed 1 in the steady state.

that there is no technical progress and that expected output remains at its current level Q_t forever, so that there will be zero net investment in the long run. Under these assumptions, the wage bill saving at time s accruing to the marginal unit of capital installed at time t i $\frac{1-\alpha}{\alpha}\bar{w}\left(\frac{Q_t}{AK_s}\right)^{1/\alpha} e^{-\delta(s-t)}$. To evaluate this expression for $s > t$ we must assume some path for the capital stock. We assume that the firm myopically ignores its own net investment so that $K_s = K_t$ for $s \geq t$. Therefore, the value of q at time t is

$$\text{(II.B.1)} \qquad \text{a.} \quad q_t = \int_t^\infty \frac{1-\alpha}{\alpha}\bar{w}\left(\frac{Q_t}{AK_t}\right)^{1/\alpha} e^{-(r+\delta)(s-t)}ds = \frac{1-\alpha}{\alpha}\bar{w}\left(\frac{Q_t}{AK_t}\right)^{1/\alpha}\frac{1}{r+\delta}$$

$$\text{b.} \qquad = \frac{1-\alpha}{\alpha}\bar{w}\frac{L_t}{K_t}\frac{1}{r+\delta}$$

Note that for any given labor capital ratio, an increase in the depreciation rate reduces the value of q_t.[1]

The dynamic properties of this partial equilibrium system can be examined if we introduce the gross investment function $I_t = I(q_t)$.

---

[1]Under the particular myopic assumption in this section, the rental price of capital is assumed constant. A higher rate of physical depreciation, thus implies a faster decline in the stream of returns accruing to an extra unit of capital installed at time t, since the capital disappears more rapidly. Under the myopic assumption that firms ignore all future gross investment so that

$$K_s = K_t e^{-\delta(s-t)},$$

the rental price of capital increases over time. Indeed, it increases fast enough so that an increase δ increases q_t, for a given labor capital ratio.

We assume that I_t has the following properties: $I(1) = 0$ and $I'(\ ) > 0$. The rate of change of the capital stock is, by definition, equal to gross investment less depreciation so that

(II.B.2) $$\dot{K}_t = I(q_t) - \delta K_t \quad .$$

Differentiating this expression with respect to K_t and noting from (II.B.1) that $\left.\frac{dq_t}{dK_t}\right|_{Q_t=\text{constant}} = -\frac{1}{\alpha}\frac{q_t}{K_t}$ we obtain

(II.B.3) $$\frac{d\dot{K}_t}{dK_t} = -\frac{1}{\alpha} I'(q) \frac{q_t}{K_t} - \delta < 0 \quad .$$

Since $\frac{d\dot{K}_t}{dK_t} < 0$ for all K_t, q_t in the positive quadrant, we know that if a steady state exists, it is unique and stable.

From (II.B.2), the steady state capital stock, if it exists, is given by the value of K for which $I(q(K)) = \delta K$. In Figure II.2, δK is a straight line through the origin with slope δ. The curve $I(q(K))$ is a decreasing function of K and crosses the horizontal axis at $\bar{K} = (\frac{1-\alpha}{\alpha})^{\alpha}(\frac{\bar{w}}{r+\delta})^{\alpha}\frac{Q}{A} > 0$ since $q(\bar{K}) = 1$. Clearly, then, $I(0) > 0$ and hence $I(q(K))$ lies above δK for $K = 0$. Since $I(q(K))$ lies below δK for $K = \bar{K}$, $I(q(I)) = \delta K$ for some K between 0 and $\bar{K}$, say K^*. But what determines K^*? For given values of the parameters α, $\bar{w}$, r, δ, and A, and for given assumptions about Q_s and K_s, the steady capital stock depends on the functional form of $I(\ )$. The functional form of $I(\ )$ in turn depends on adjustment or installation costs. Lower installation costs raise the rate of investment, $I(q)$, for any value of $q > 1$. The dotted line in figure II.2 represents

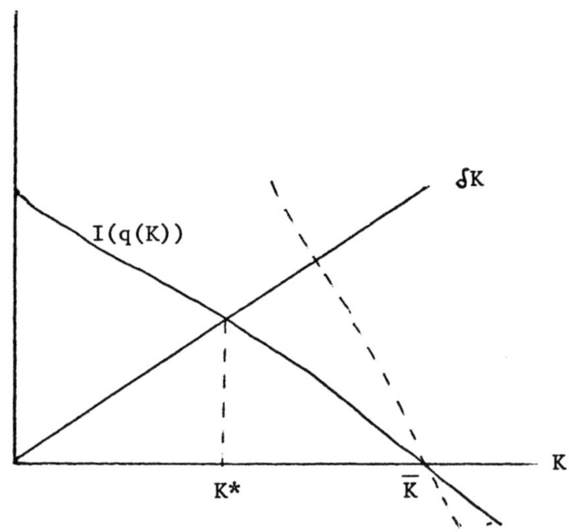

Figure II.2

lower installation costs than the solid line and indicates a higher steady state capital stock. In the limiting case of zero adjustment costs, there is instantaneous adjustment and the steady state capital stock is equal to $\bar{K} = \left(\frac{1-\alpha}{\alpha} \right)^{\alpha} \left(\frac{\bar{w}}{r+\delta} \right)^{\alpha} \frac{\bar{Q}}{A}$.[1] The effect of an increase in the rate of depreciation is to shift the I(q(K)) curve leftward, thereby reducing $\bar{K}$. In addition, the δK line is rotated counter-clockwise through the origin. The net effect is to lower the steady state capital stock.

C. Taxes, Depreciation Allowance, and the Investment Tax Credit

We now incorporate taxes into the analysis, but still within the framework of myopic optimization. Assume once again that output is expected to grow at the exponential rate g and that there is Harrod-neutral technical progress at rate λ. Let τ be the corporate tax rate, and k_t be the investment tax credit rate on the purchase on new capital goods.[2] The investment tax credit reduces the depreciation base of an asset by the amount of the credit.[3] Let D(s−t) be

---

[1]In the absence of depreciation, the steady state capital stock is independent of the costs of adjustment since steady state gross investment is zero in this case. As long as I(1) = 0 and I'( ) > 0, the steady state capital stock will be that value of K for which q = 1, namely, $K = \left(\frac{1-\alpha}{\alpha} \right)^{\alpha} \left(\frac{\bar{w}}{r}\right)^{\alpha} \frac{\bar{Q}}{A}$.)

[2]We assume that there is no credit against installation costs; indeed, in this section, we implicitly assume that installation costs are neither tax-deductible as current expense, nor are they capitalized into the book value of the asset and depreciated over time. We correct this in section III.

[3]See footnote 2, page 39.

the per unit accounting depreciation at time s for a unit of capital installed at time t.[1] Following Hall and Jorgenson (1967), we let z_t be the present value of the depreciation deductions for an asset bought at time t so that $z_t = \int_t^{\infty} D(s-t)e^{-r(s-t)}ds$.

The production function, with Harrod-neutral technical change, is $Q_s = A(e^{\lambda(s-t)}L_s)^{\alpha}K_s^{1-\alpha}$ so that the marginal rate of substitution is $\frac{1-\alpha}{\alpha}\left(\frac{Q_s}{AK_s}\right)^{1/\alpha} e^{-\lambda(s-t)}$. Hence, the after-tax wage saving at time s accruing to the undepreciated portion of a unit of capital installed at time t is

$$\text{(II.C.1)} \qquad (1-\tau)\bar{w}\,\frac{1-\alpha}{\alpha}\left(\frac{Q_s}{AK_s}\right)^{1/\alpha} e^{-(\delta+\lambda)(s-t)}$$

Now observe that $Q_s = Q_t e^{g(s-t)}$. We continue with the myopic assumption that firms ignore future net investment so that $K_s = K_t$, $s \geq t$. Making these substitutions into (II.C.1), we obtain[2]

$$\text{(II.C.2)} \quad q_t = \int_t^{\infty} (1-\tau)\bar{w}\,\frac{1-\alpha}{\alpha}\,\frac{L_t}{K_t}\, e^{-(\delta+\lambda-\frac{g}{\alpha})(s-t)}e^{-r(s-t)}ds + \tau(1-k_t)z_t + k_t .$$

Performing the integration, we obtain the following expression for q_t

$$\text{(II.C.3)} \quad q_t = (1-\tau)\bar{w}\,\frac{1-\alpha}{\alpha}\,\frac{L_t}{K_t}\,\frac{1}{r+\delta+\lambda-\frac{g}{\alpha}} + \tau(1-k_t)z_t + k_t$$

Thus we have

---

[1] Note that $\int_0^{\infty} D(u)du = 1$.

[2] We now interpret r as the after-tax discount rate.

$$q_t = q(\underset{?}{\tau}, \underset{+}{\bar{w}}, \underset{+}{\frac{L_t}{K_t}}, \underset{-}{r}, \underset{-}{\lambda}, \underset{+}{g}, \underset{-}{\delta}, \underset{+}{k_t}, \underset{+}{z_t}) \tag{II.C.4}$$

where the sign of the partial derivative of q with respect to each argument is given in parentheses below the argument.[1] Except for $\frac{\partial q_t}{\partial \tau}$, whose sign is indeterminate, all partial derivatives are of the expected sign. Especially interesting is the fact that an increase in the investment tax credit would increase q_t and hence would increase current investment. The unsettling feature of this analysis is that as far as q_t and current investment are concerned, there is no difference between a temporary investment tax credit and a permanent investment tax credit. One would think that a temporary tax credit would have a larger impact effect than a permanent tax credit because the decline in the tax credit over time would induce intertemporal shifting of investment expenditures. This effect does not appear in our analysis because of the myopia assumed on the part of firms. They do not anticipate future net investment and would not see the benefit to be gained from the intertemporal shifting of investment expenditure. In the next section we move on to a forward-looking analysis and in Section VI we study the effects of temporary and permanent investment tax credits.

III. Intertemporal Investment Decisions

In Section II, the calculation of q_t required knowledge of the

[1]The signs of these derivatives are based on the assumption that τ, k_t, and z_t all lie between 0 and 1, inclusive.

future path of the capital stock. We arbitrarily assumed that firms myopically ignored future net investment and based investment plans at time t on the assumption that $K_s = K_t$, for $s \geq t$. This arbitrary assumption provided us with analytic simplicity. However, the assumed myopia of firms led to the unsettling result that variations in the duration of an investment tax credit have no effect on the current rate of investment. In this section we drop the myopic assumption about the path of the capital stock and analyze investment behavior by a method which does not require explicit knowledge of the path of the capital stock.

We first examine a simple case without taxes or technical progress in which output is expected to remain constant at $\bar{Q}$. The wage saving at time s from an extra unit of capital installed at time t is the product of the wage rate, the marginal rate of substitution of labor for capital and the undepreciated portion of the unit of capital remaining at time s. Hence, we calculate q_t as

$$q_t = \frac{1-\alpha}{\alpha} \bar{w} \int_t^{\infty} \left(\frac{\bar{Q}}{AK_s} \right)^{1/\alpha} e^{-(r+\delta)(s-t)} ds \tag{III.1}$$

The dynamic properties of this system may be studied by differentiating both sides of (III.1) with respect to time to obtain[1]

---

[1]This equation is the same as equation 2 of Hall and Jorgenson (1967) if we set their rental rate c equal to

$$\frac{1-\alpha}{\alpha} \bar{w} \frac{L_t}{K_t} = \frac{1-\alpha}{\alpha} \bar{w} \left(\frac{Q_t}{AK_t} \right)^{1/\alpha} .$$

$$\text{(III.2)} \quad \text{a.} \quad \dot{q}_t = -\frac{1-\alpha}{\alpha}\,\bar{w}\left(\frac{\bar{Q}}{AK_t}\right)^{1/\alpha} + (r+\delta)q_t$$

$$\text{b.} \quad = -\frac{1-\alpha}{\alpha}\,\bar{w}\,\frac{L_t}{K_t} + (r+\delta)q_t$$

Equation (III.2) is a differential equation governing the movement of q. The differential equation for K is

$$\text{(III.3)} \qquad \dot{K} = I(q) - \delta K,$$

where I( ) is the gross investment function with I(1) = 0 and $I' \geq 0$. The phase diagram for this system is shown in figure III.1. The slope of the locus of points for which $\dot{q} = 0$ is

$$\left.\frac{dq}{dK}\right|_{\dot{q}=0} = -\frac{\frac{1-\alpha}{\alpha^2}\,\bar{w}\left(\frac{\bar{Q}}{A}\right)^{1/\alpha} K_t^{-\frac{1}{\alpha}-1}}{r+\delta} < 0 ,$$

and the slope of the locus for which $\dot{K} = 0$ is

$$\left.\frac{dq}{dK}\right|_{\dot{K}=0} = \frac{\delta}{I'} > 0 .$$

Note that the q-intercept of the $\dot{K} = 0$ locus is at q = 1 since with zero capital stock, there is no required replacement investment so that q = 1. This phase diagram can be interpreted in two ways. It may be interpreted as showing that the system has no stable equilibrium. Alternatively, this phase diagram may be interpreted as showing the

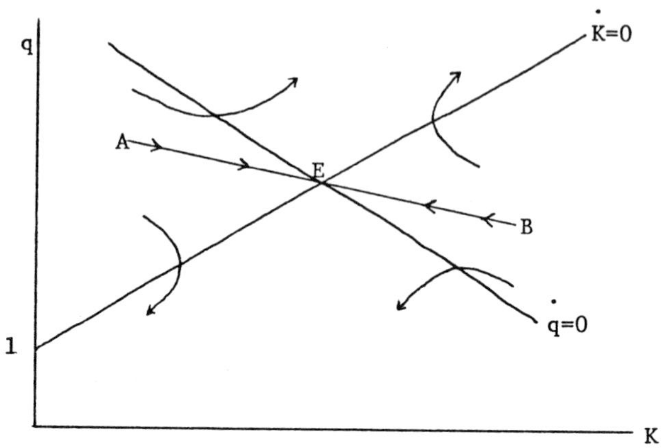

Figure III.1

unique perfect foresight path to equilibrium. If this system is not to blow up asymptotically, then the state vector (K, q) must lie on AE or BE. The position of (K, q) at any point of time is determined by the existing level of the capital stock.

Now, in the absence of myopia on the part of firms, we can examine how an increase in the rate of depreciation affects the steady state equilibrium. From equation (III.3), we see that an increase in δ increases the slope of $\dot{K} = 0$ so that this locus rotates counter-clockwise around its intercept q = 1, as shown in Figure III.2. Essentially, for any positive level of capital stock, a higher rate of replacement investment is necessary. This higher equilibrium rate of gross investment is induced by a higher q. The increase in δ shifts the $\dot{q} = 0$ schedule downward since at any level of K, the marginal value of capital is reduced. These effects indicate that a higher rate of depreciation is associated with a lower steady state capital stock, as in the myopic analysis of Section II. The effect on steady state q depends on whether δK, the steady state rate of replacement

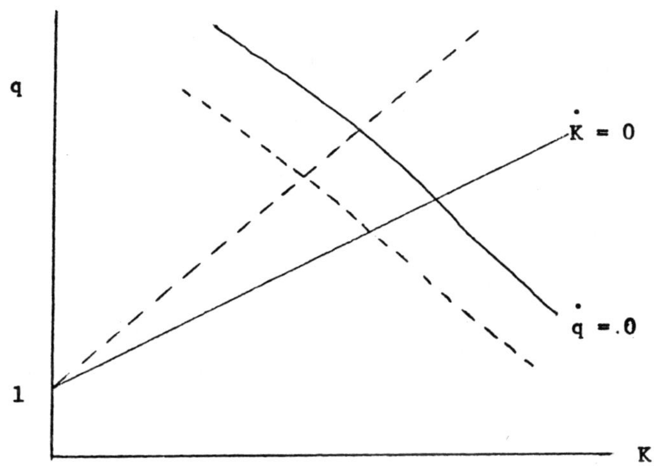

Figure III.2

investment, increases or decreases.[1]

We may also use the phase diagram apparatus to examine the reactions to exogenous disturbances from an initial steady state equilibrium. Assume that we are in steady state equilibrium at point E_o in figure III.3 and that the expected level of output increases from $\bar{Q}$ to Q_1. This increase will not affect the $\dot{K} = 0$ schedule but shifts the $\dot{q} = 0$ locus rightward. Hence, the market value of installed

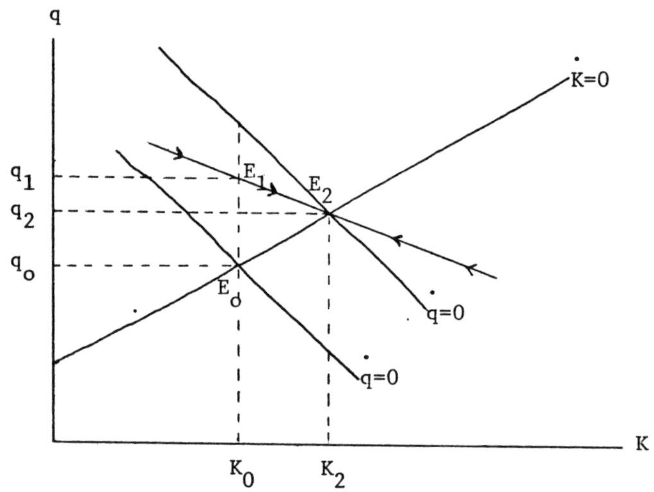

Figure III.3

capital jumps immediately to q_1, inducing a higher rate of gross investment. As the capital stock accumulates toward K_2, the value of q falls toward q_2. The new steady state equilibrium is at E_2. The higher capital stock at E_2 implies a greater amount of depreciation than at E_o. In order to induce the higher level of gross necessary to have zero net

---

[1]Note that in the absence of depreciation, the $\dot{K} = 0$ locus is horizontal at q = 1. The steady state capital stock is given by that level of K for which q = 1, regardless of the installation costs which underlie the investment function. In this case the steady state is characterized by zero gross investment.

investment, a higher level of q is required.[1]

We now incorporate taxes, accounting depreciation, and the investment tax credit into our analysis. We assume that the book value of a new unit of capital is q_t and proceed as in subsection II.C. By analogy with (II.C.2), we write:[2]

$$(III.4) \qquad q_t = (1-\tau)\,\frac{1-\alpha}{\alpha}\,\bar{w}\int_t^{\infty}\left(\frac{\bar{Q}}{AK_s}\right)^{1/\alpha} e^{-(r+\delta)(s-t)}ds + q_t(1-k_t)\tau z_t + k_t q_t \; .$$

Differentiating (III.4) with respect to time, we obtain

$$(III.5) \qquad \dot{q}_t = -\,\frac{(1-\tau)}{(1-k)(1-\tau z)}\;\frac{1-\alpha}{\alpha}\,\bar{w}\,\frac{L_t}{K_t} + (r+\delta)q_t \; .$$

From this result we may easily obtain the Hall-Jorgenson expression for the rental cost of capital (their equation 6), $c = q(r+\delta)\,\frac{(1-k)(1-\tau z)}{(1-\tau)}$.

---

[1]This is due to the fact that adjustment costs are an increasing function of gross investment. If adjustment costs were a function of I/K, then the $\dot{K} = 0$ schedule would be horizontal and the exogenous change in expected output would not change q in the steady state. Even in this case, the steady state is not invariant to adjustment costs because the level of q at which $\dot{K} = 0$ is horizontal depends on installation costs.

[2]The present value of the depreciation allowance is calculated under the assumption that the depreciation base is reduced by the amount of the investment tax credit as called for by the Long Amendment. After the Long Amendment was repealed in 1964, the investment tax credit was no longer subtracted from the depreciation base so that the present value of the depreciation allowance is $q_t \tau z_t$.

Setting $\dot{q}_t$ equal to zero and noting that $\bar{w}L/\alpha = Q$, we obtain

$$\text{(III.6)} \qquad K = (1-\alpha)Q\,\frac{1-\tau}{q(r+\delta)(1-k)(1-\tau z)}$$

which is the Hall-Jorgenson expression for the desired stock of capital.

To examine the effects of an exogenous change, assume that we are initially at the steady state equilibrium in figure III.4. If any of the parameters k, τ, z, or r jumps instantaneously, then the $\dot{q} = 0$ locus shifts instantaneously. However, the $\dot{K} = 0$ locus is not affected by such shifts. Increases in k or z will shift the $\dot{q} = 0$ locus upward in figure III.4, whereas decreases in r or in τ will shift this locus

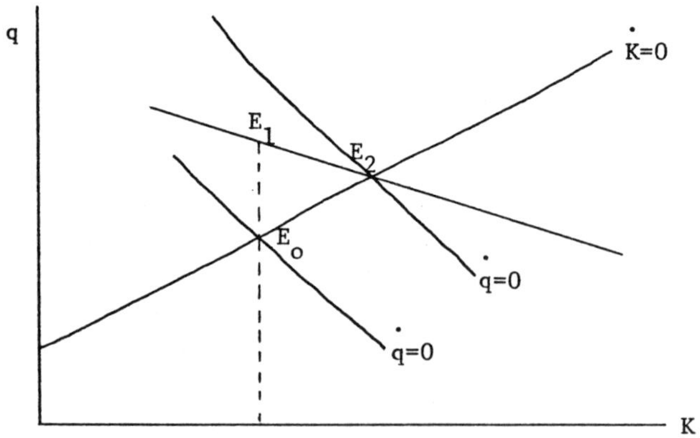

Figure III.4

upward.[1] Any of these changes will cause an instantaneous jump in q

---

[1]A decrease in τ shifts the $\dot{q} = 0$ locus upward since $\frac{\partial}{\partial\tau}[\frac{1-\tau}{1-\tau z}] = -\frac{(1-z)}{(1-\tau z)^2} < 0$, as long as $z < 1$. We have assumed that the before-tax discount rate adjusts so as to keep the after-tax discount rate r constant.

and an increase in investment. Net investment will occur and q will decline until the new steady state is reached at E_2.

In this section we have discussed only permanent changes which occur when the system is in long-run equilibrium. In Section VI, we expand the analysis to examine temporary as well as permanent changes which occur when the system is at any point along the path to steady state equilibrium. Before that, however, we explicitly discuss the role of installation costs in Section IV and show that the steady state results obtained from the q approach may be derived from explicit intertemporal optimization in Section V.

IV. Installation Costs

We have made reference to adjustment or installation cost as the fundamental reason why the rate of investment is an increasing function of q. In this section we sketch a derivation of the investment function from adjustment costs. In our one-sector model, the investing firm can buy capital goods at the price of output, which is assumed to be one. When the firm installs the capital in place, the piece of capital has a value q. If q exceeds one, the firm would want to buy the capital good and install it immediately, if there were no installation costs. However, there are costs due to the installation of capital and it is reasonable to assume that per unit installation costs increase with the rate of installation. Therefore, installation costs are an increasing convex function of the rate of investment. Since the purchase price of uninstalled capital goods is constant, the adjustment cost, i.e., the cost of purchasing and installing capital, is an increasing convex function of the rate of investment.

The case for convex adjustment cost was made quite strongly by Eisner and Strotz (1963). The per unit adjustment costs may be expected to rise with the rate of investment due to factors external to the firm and to factors internal to the firm. One such external factor is that the firm might face a rising flow supply curve of capital goods as a result of monopsony power in the capital goods market. Even if the firm is a competitor in this market, Eisner and Strotz argue that the representative firm will recognize that other firms in the industry will have the same investment plans and that the price of capital goods will be bid up by the entire industry when investment is proceeding at a rapid pace. This argument is somewhat shaky as it depends on how an individual firm's actions are linked to the actions of other firms in its industry and on how the firm views these links. However, there are reasonable sets of assumptions which make this argument valid. As for internal costs of adjustment, we would expect a convex investment cost function for vertically integrated firms whose capital-producing segment has a rising short-run marginal cost curve. Even if the firm is not vertically integrated, and buys its capital from other firms at a fixed price, it might have to pay its own workers to install the capital. In order to speed up the installation of a given increment of capital, the firm would have to pay a higher installation cost. That is, a higher rate of installation is achieved with a higher per unit cost. In this essay, we assume that the price of uninstalled capital is equal to one (in our one-sector world), and that the installation cost function is an increasing convex function of the rate of investment. Hence, the total cost of purchasing capital and installing it in place is an increasing convex function of the rate of investment.[1]

We examine an infinitesimal time period dt. During this interval, the gross addition to the capital stock is Idt and the value to the firm of this gross investment is qIdt. The total cost is equal to the purchase price of the uninstalled capital goods plus the installation costs. We assume that installation costs incurred during dt are an increasing function of the rate of investment c(I)dt. The assumption that per unit installation costs increase with the rate of investment implies that $c'(\ ) > 0$. We make the further assumption that $c''(\ ) > 0$, so that marginal installation cost is a positive and increasing function of the rate of investment. Now the total purchase and installation cost during dt is $(I + c(I))dt$. The optimal rate of investment is that rate for which marginal value equals marginal cost, i.e., that rate for which $q = 1 + c'(I)$. Hence, we may write $I(q) = c'^{-1}(q-1)$. Since $c'(\ )$ is an increasing function, $c'^{-1}(q)$ is an increasing function of q. Furthermore, we assume that $c'(0) = 0$ so that $c'^{-1}(0) = 0$. Therefore, I(q) is an increasing function of q with $I(1) = 0$.

In dealing with growth models, it may be more reasonable to assume that per unit installation costs are a function of the rate of investment relative to the stock of capital. Let $c^*(I/K)$ be the per unit cost of installation at rate I during the interval dt, with the assumptions that $c^*(0) = 0$, $c^{*\prime}(I) > 0$, and $c^{*\prime\prime}(I) > 0$. Therefore, total installation costs during dt are $c^*(I/K)Idt$. Setting the marginal value of I equal to its marginal cost, we obtain $q = 1 + c^*(I/K) + (I/K)c^{*\prime}(I/K)$.

Note that the marginal cost is a function of (I/K)

---

[1]Although Eisner and Strotz acknowledge that the adjustment cost function might not be convex over certain ranges of the rate of investment, they nonetheless adopt the convexity assumption. This assumption has also been adopted by Lucas (1967a), Gould (1969), and Treadway (1969). Rothschild (1971) discusses the implications of nonconvex costs of adjustment.

so we may write $q = 1 + c(I/K)$, where $c(I/K) = c^*(I/K) + (I/K)c^{*\prime}(I/K)$ with $c'(\ ) > 0$ and $c(0) = 0$. By analogous reasoning to that above, we obtain, $q - 1 = c(I/K)$. Hence, $I/K(q) = c^{-1}(q-1)$ with the properties that $(I/K)' > 0$ and $(I/K)(1) = 0$.

As mentioned earlier, this alternative form of the investment function is useful when examining growth models. Assume that output is expected to grow at the exponential rate g and that per unit installation costs, c^*, are a function of I/K. In addition, we ignore the effect of taxes. Thus, we obtain

$$\text{(IV.1)} \quad q_t = \int_t^\infty \bar{w}\frac{1-\alpha}{\alpha} A^{-\frac{1}{\alpha}} \left(\frac{Q_s}{K_s}\right)^{-\frac{1}{\alpha}} e^{-(r+\delta)(s-t)} ds + \int_t^\infty \left(\frac{I_s}{K_s}\right)^2 c^{*\prime}\left(\frac{I_s}{K_s}\right) e^{-(r+\delta)(s-t)} ds.$$

The first term in this expression is analogous to (III.1). The second term on the right hand side represents the present value of the installation cost savings due to an extra unit of capital installed at time t. The total installation cost at any point of time is $Ic^*(I/K)$ so that the cost saving from an extra unit of capital is $(I/K)^2 c^{*\prime}(I/K)$. If the extra unit of capital is installed at time t, then the installation cost saving at time s, $s > t$, is $(I/K)^2 c^{*\prime}(I/K) e^{-\delta(s-t)}$. Hence, the last term in (IV.1) represents the present value of installation cost savings accruing to an additional unit of capital installed at time t. Differentiating (IV.1) with respect to time, we obtain

$$\text{(IV.2)} \quad \dot{q}_t = (r+\delta) q_t - \frac{1-\alpha}{\alpha} \bar{w} A^{-\frac{1}{\alpha}} \left(\frac{Q_t}{K_t}\right)^{-\frac{1}{\alpha}} - \left(\frac{I_t}{K_t}\right)^2 c^{*\prime}\left(\frac{I_t}{K_t}\right).$$

This equation describes the movement of q_t over time as a function of the capital output ratio and q_t. (Recall that I/K can be expressed as a function of q_t) The rate of change of the capital output ratio may be expressed as $\dot{K/Q} = (K/Q)(\dot{K}/K - \dot{Q}/Q)$. Substituting $\frac{I}{K}(q) - \delta$ for $\dot{K}/K$, and recalling that $\dot{Q}/Q = g$, we obtain the second equation of motion of our system

$$(IV.3) \qquad \dot{\overline{K/Q}} = (K/Q)(\frac{I}{K}(q) - (g+\delta)) .$$

The $\dot{q} = 0$ locus is downward sloping in the neighborhood of steady state equilibrium.[1] The $\dot{\overline{K/Q}} = 0$ locus, for $K > 0$, is horizontal at q^*, where q^* is defined so that $\frac{I}{K}(q^*) = \delta + g$. Note that since $\delta + g > 0$, $q^* > 1$. The phase diagram for this system is shown in Figure IV.1. The $\dot{\overline{K/Q}} = 0$ locus uniquely determines the level of q. Given the level of q, say q^*, the steady state capital output ratio is determined from the $\dot{q} = 0$ locus.

V. Explicit Intertemporal Optimization

We have argued in previous sections that investment is a function of q. When q exceeds 1, there is a demand for an instantaneous jump in the capital stock and hence there would be a demand for additional capital as quickly as possible. However, convex installation costs prevent an instantaneous increase in the capital stock and lead to finite rates of investment. A more direct approach to determine the path of the capital stock is to maximize directly the present value of the firm's net cash flow, recognizing the cash outlays for the purchase of capital goods and their installation.

---

[1]Since $\frac{\partial \dot{q}}{\partial (Q/K)} > 0$, the slope of the $\dot{q} = 0$ locus has the opposite sign of $\partial\dot{q}/\partial q$. Ignoring installation cost savings, $\partial\dot{q}/\partial q = r + \delta > 0$ so that the $\dot{q} = 0$ locus is downward sloping. However, taking account of installation cost savings, $\frac{\partial \dot{q}}{\partial q} = r + \delta - (2\frac{I}{K}c^{*\prime} + (\frac{I}{K})^2 c^{*\prime\prime}) \frac{d(I/K)}{dq} = r + \delta - \frac{I}{K}$. So long as the steady state growth rate of capital, $(I/K) - \delta$, does not exceed the discount rate r (a necessary condition for q to be finite), $\partial\dot{q}/\partial q > 0$. Hence, $\dot{q} = 0$ is downward sloping in the neighborhood of the steady state.

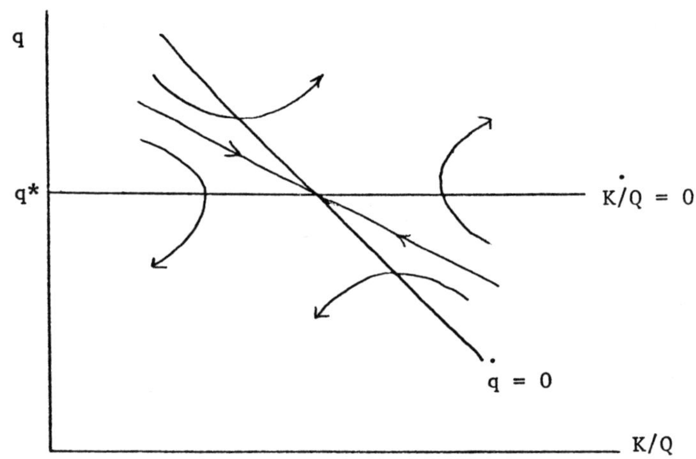

Figure IV.1

First we consider the case where output is expected to remain constant at Q_0. The after-tax operating cash flow in the interval dt is

$$(Q_0 - \bar{w}\,(\frac{Q_0}{A})^{\frac{1}{\alpha}}\, K^{1-\frac{1}{\alpha}})(1-\tau)dt \ .$$

The cost of installing new capital at rate I is (I + c(I))dt, where c(I) is total installation cost in dt. The investment tax credit at rate k produces k(I + c(I))dt in tax savings if installation costs are capitalized into the value of the capital. Recall that z is the present value of the depreciation allowance deduction per unit value of capital, so that $\tau z(1-k)(I + c(I))dt$ is the total present value of the depreciation benefit acquired in dt. Putting together all of these components of cash flow, we obtain

$$\text{(V.1)}\quad \int_0^{\infty} [(Q_o-\bar{w}(\frac{Q_o}{A})^{\frac{1}{\alpha}}\, K_t^{1-\frac{1}{\alpha}})(1-\tau)-(I+c(I))+k(I+c(I))+\tau z(1-k)(I+c(I))]e^{-rt}dt$$

We wish to maximize (V.1) with respect ot I, subject to the constraint that $\dot{K} = I - \delta K$. The Hamiltonian for this problem is

$$\text{(V.2)}\quad H=e^{-rt}\{(Q_o-\bar{w}(\frac{Q_o}{A})^{\frac{1}{\alpha}}\, K^{1-\frac{1}{\alpha}})(1-\tau) - (1-k)(1-\tau z)(I+c(I)) + P_K(I-\delta K)\}$$

where P_K is the costate variable (Lagrange multiplier) corresponding to the marginal value of capital. Solving the first-order condition $\partial H/\partial I=0$, we obtain

$$\text{(V.3)}\qquad c'(I) = \frac{P_K}{(1-k)(1-\tau z)} - 1 \ .$$

Since $c'' > 0$, (V.3) indicates that investment is an increasing function of $P_K/(1-k)(1-\tau z)$. But $P_K/(1-k)(1-\tau z)$ is equal to q as defined earlier, since P_K is the marginal value of an additional unit of installed capital and $(1-k)(1-\tau z)$ is the tax-adjusted price of uninstalled capital goods. Hence (V.3) implies that investment is an increasing function of q.

The identity of $P_K/(1-k)(1-\tau z)$ with q may also be seen by solving the necessary condition $\frac{d}{dt}(P_K e^{-rt}) = -\frac{\partial H}{\partial K}$ to obtain

$$(V.4) \qquad \dot{P}_K = (r+\delta)P_K - \frac{1-\alpha}{\alpha} w \left(\frac{Q_o}{AK}\right)^{1/\alpha} (1-\tau).$$

Dividing both sides of (V.4) by $(1-k)(1-\tau z)$ and assuming that $(1-k)(1-\tau z)$ is constant over time, we obtain

$$(V.5) \qquad \dot{q} = (r+\delta)q - \frac{1-\alpha}{\alpha} w \frac{1-\tau}{(1-k)(1-\tau z)} \left(\frac{Q_o}{AK}\right)^{1/\alpha}$$

which is identical to (III.5) with $(Q_o/AK)^{1/\alpha}$ replacing L/K.

To determine the steady state capital stock, we set $\dot{P}_K=0$ in (V.4), (or equivalently, $\dot{q}=0$ in (V.5)), to obtain

$$(V.6) \qquad K = \frac{(1-\alpha)Q(1-\tau)}{(r+\delta)P_K} = \frac{(1-\alpha)Q(1-\tau)}{q(r+\delta)(1-k)(1-\tau z)},$$

which is identical to (III.6).

We may also apply this analysis to the case with a constant rate of output growth. In this case, the total investment cost during dt is $(1 + c^*(I/K))I\,dt$, where $c^*(I/K)$ is the per unit installation cost. The present value of the cash flow is

$$(V.7) \qquad \int_o^\infty \{(Q_t - \bar{w}(\frac{Q_t}{A})^{1/\alpha} K_t^{1-1/\alpha})(1-\tau) - (1-\tau z)(1-k)(1+c^*(\frac{I}{K}))I\}\, e^{-rt} dt.$$

We must choose I to maximize (V.7) subject to $\dot{K} = I - \delta K$. Again using the maximum principle and setting the partial derivative of the Hamiltonian with respect to I equal to zero, we obtain

$$(V.8) \qquad 1 + c^*(\frac{I}{K}) + \frac{I}{K}c^{*\prime}(\frac{I}{K}) = \frac{P_K}{(1-k)(1-\tau z)} = q,$$

where P_K is the shadow price of capital goods in place, as explained above. Thus, the marginal cost of increasing the rate of investment is set equal to q. Since the marginal cost is an increasing function of I/K, the investment capital ratio is an increasing function of q.

Now we solve the necessary condition $\frac{d(P_K e^{-rt})}{dt} = -\frac{\partial H}{\partial K}$ to obtain

$$(V.9) \qquad \dot{P}_K = (r+\delta)P_K - \frac{1-\alpha}{\alpha} \bar{w}\left(\frac{Q_t}{AK_t}\right)^{1/\alpha} (1-\tau) - (1-k)(1-\tau z)\left(\frac{I}{K}\right)^2 c^{*\prime}\left(\frac{I}{K}\right).$$

Now dividing (V.9) by $(1-k)(1-\tau z)$ and assuming that $(1-k)(1-\tau z)$ does not change over time, we obtain

$$\text{(V.10)} \quad \dot{q}_t = (r+\delta)q_t - \frac{1-\tau}{(1-k)(1-\tau z)} \frac{1-\alpha}{\alpha} \bar{w} \left(\frac{Q_t}{AK_t}\right)^{\frac{1}{\alpha}} - \left(\frac{I}{K}\right)^2 c^{*\prime}\left(\frac{I}{K}\right) .$$

Observe that, except for the tax parameters which were ignored in Section IV, (V.10) is identical to (IV.2). Hence, in this section, we have shown that the q approach discussed heuristically earlier can be rigorously derived from explicit intertemporal optimizing behavior.

VI. The Effects of Anticipated Exogenous Changes on Investment

In Section III, we examined the effects of unanticipated exogenous changes from an initial position of steady state equilibrium. In this section we shall broaden the analysis along two dimensions. First we shall examine anticipated exogenous shocks. In a perfect foresight model, all future shocks are anticipated since the entire future is known. The only unanticipated changes are surprise shocks that occur in the present. Essentially, the distinction between unanticipated and anticipated shocks has as its analogue in perfect foresight models the distinction between present and future changes. The second new aspect in the analysis of this section is that we no longer assume that we are initially in long-run equilibrium when a shock occurs. We assume only that initially we are on the stable path to long-run equilibrium.

A. An Anticipated Increase in Output

Suppose we are initially at time t_o, and that output has been expected to remain at Q_o forever. Therefore the economy is on the stable path leading to E_o (see Figure VI.A.1). Its position on this path is determined by the current level of the capital stock K_{t_o}. Now, suppose that expectations change so that output is expected to jump to $Q_1 > Q_o$ at some future time $t_1 > t_o$ and to remain at that level forever. Hence, the expected values of output are $Q_s = Q_o$ for $t_o \leq s \leq t_1$, and $Q_s = Q_1$ for $s > t_1$. Now, for $t \leq t_1$, we have, by analogy with (III.4),

$$(1-k)(1-\tau z)q_t = (1-\tau)\frac{1-\alpha}{\alpha}\bar{w}\left[\int_t^{t_1}\left(\frac{Q_o}{A}\right)^{\frac{1}{\alpha}} K_s^{-\frac{1}{\alpha}} e^{-(r+\delta)(s-t)}ds + \int_{t_1}^{\infty}\left(\frac{Q_1}{A}\right)^{\frac{1}{\alpha}} K_s^{-\frac{1}{\alpha}} e^{-(r+\delta)(s-t)}ds\right] . \tag{VI.A.1}$$

Differentiating (VI.A.1) with respect to time, we obtain the equation of motion for q_t,

$$\dot{q}_t = \frac{-(1-\tau)}{(1-k)(1-\tau z)}\frac{1-\alpha}{\alpha}\bar{w}\left(\frac{Q_o}{AK_t}\right)^{1/\alpha} + (r+\delta)q_t \tag{VI.A.2}$$

Note that the anticipation of a change in output does not affect the equation of motion for $t < t_1$. This does not imply that there is no effect on q_t and hence $I(q_t)$. As will be seen below, the anticipated increase in output will cause a discrete jump in q_t and in $I(q_t)$. However, after this immediate jump in q_t, the initial laws of motion apply until time t_1. That is, for any point in K,q space, the vector of motion $(\dot{K}_t, \dot{q}_t)$ is unchanged by the anticipation of a future increase in output.

After the change in output occurs, that is, for $t > t_1$, we have

$$\text{(VI.A.3)} \qquad (1-k)(1-\tau z)q_t = \frac{1-\alpha}{\alpha}\bar{w}\int_t^{\infty}\left(\frac{Q_1}{AK_t}\right)^{1/\alpha} e^{-(r+\delta)(s-t)}ds$$

Hence, for $t > t_1$, the past values of output do not directly affect the value of q_t. Given the current level of K_t, neither past values of the level of output, nor changes in the level of output, have an effect on the current or future rates of investment. All adjustment to an anticipated change takes place prior to the actual change. Finally, note that after t_1, the equation of motion for q_t is

$$\text{(VI.A.4)} \qquad \dot{q}_t = -\frac{(1-\tau)}{(1-k)(1-\tau z)}\frac{1-\alpha}{\alpha}\bar{w}\left(\frac{Q_1}{AK_t}\right)^{1/\alpha} + (r+\delta)q_t$$

Hence,, the $\dot{q} = 0$ locus shifts upwards after the increase in output at time t_1.

The effects of an anticipated jump in output are illustrated in Figure VI.A.1. The stable path and the $\dot{q} = 0$ locus corresponding to the initial output level Q_o are shown intersecting the $\dot{K} = 0$ locus at

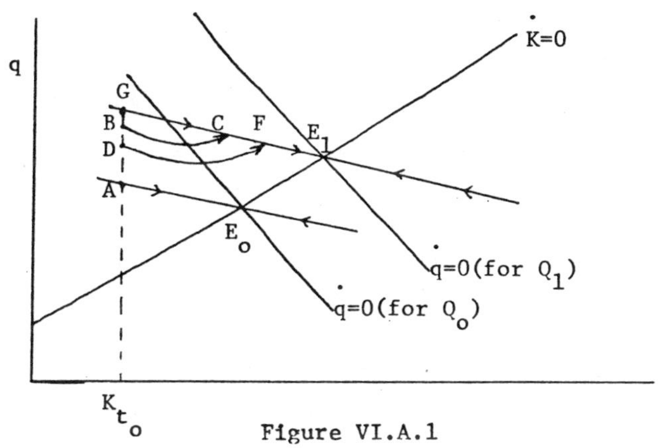

Figure VI.A.1

E_o. The stable path and the $\dot{q} = 0$ locus corresponding to the new output level are shown intersecting $\dot{K} = 0$ at E_1. Suppose that we are initially at point A on the path to long-run equilibrium when the anticipation of increased output first appears. The system immediately jumps to point B with a higher level of q. The discrete jump in q reflects the increased future wage bill savings provided by capital in the production of an increased level of output. The higher level of q increases the current rate of investment so that the time path of the capital stock responds in advance of the increase in output. Since there are convex installation costs, the response to increased output is spread out over time. The system moves smoothly along BC arriving at point C when the increase in output actually occurs (time t_1). Then the system moves smoothly along the new stable path to the long-run equilibrium at E_1.

We note that after the initial response to a change in anticipations, the system (K, q) must move continuously throughout the future. Clearly, K must move continuously at all points of time, if we impose the reasonable restriction that the rate of investment is always finite (this restriction is an implication of convex installation costs.) As for q, there must be no anticipated jumps in the market valuation of capital (the numerator of q), since in well-functioning capital markets there can be no anticipated windfall capital gains. Therefore, the numerator of q must move continuously throughout the future. The denominator of q is identically equal to 1. Therefore, q moves continuously throughout the future.[1] We have thus ruled out

---

[1] Later, when we discuss the investment tax credit, the denominator of q will differ from 1, and may change discontinuously. However, the numerator of q will never have anticipated discontinuities.

anticipated jumps in q. Any jumps in q must be unanticipated, which in this perfect foresight model, means that jumps in q can occur only at the present, when a surprise occurs.

Observe in Figure VI.A.1 that a shorter length of time is required to traverse BC than to traverse DF since along BC there is a higher rate of investment but a lower terminal capital stock.[1] Hence, the shorter is the time span until output increases, the larger is the current capital gain and the larger is the jump in the rate of investment. As a limiting case, if the increase in output is expected to occur immediately, the system moves immediately to the new stable path with q_t jumping immediately to G.

By starting from positions along the stable path other than in long-run equilibrium, we introduce more variety into the observed behavior of q_t and K_t. Neither q_t nor K_t need move monotonically to long-run equilibrium. We may identify four ranges of values of K_{t_o}, shown as zones I, II, III, and IV in Figure VI.A.2, which yield different types of paths to long-run equilibrium. For example, if K_{t_o} is in zone I, K_t increases monotonically to long-run equilibrium. However, after its initial discrete jump, q_t may either decline monotonically to equilibrium, or it may first decline, then rise, and finally fall to long-run equilibrium. In zone III, q_t first jumps discretely, then rises smoothly and finally falls smoothly to long-run equilibrium. If output is expected to rise sufficiently soon, K_t rises monotonically. However, if the anticipated rise in output is sufficiently far in the future, K_t first falls and then rises to long-run equilibrium.

---

[1]This line of argument was taken from Krugman (1977).

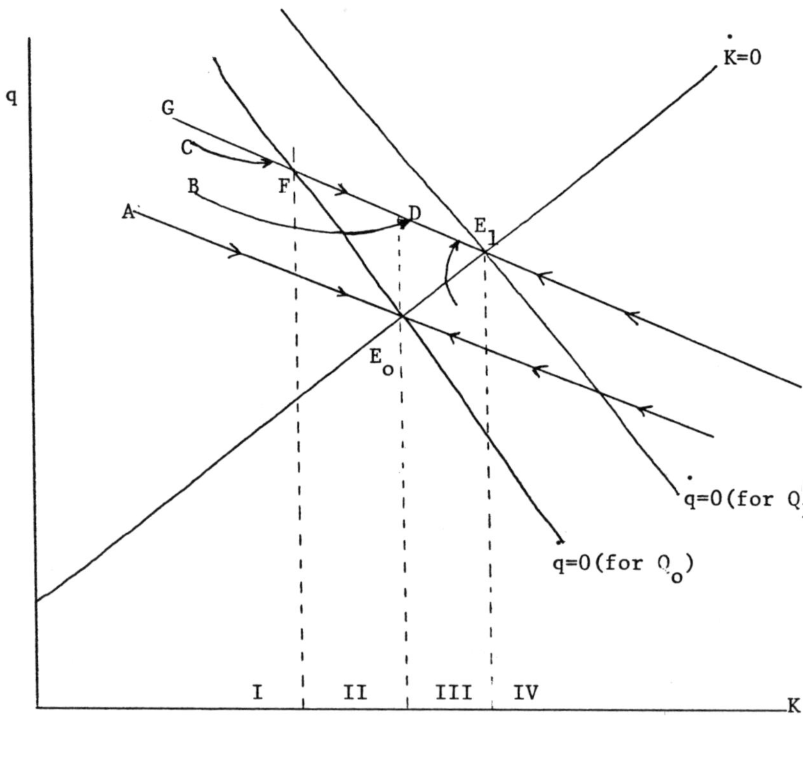

Figure VI.A.2

B. The Investment Tax Credit

We next turn to the investment tax credit (ITC) which is a very specialized policy tool to stimulate investment. In addition to its practical policy importance, the study of the ITC raises some interesting methodological issues. The comparison of a temporary vs. a permanent ITC is readily studied within the framework of anticipated and unanticipated exogenous shocks. The analysis of a temporary ITC points up a problem with our definition of the market value of capital since the condition that there be no anticipated windfall capital gains would be violated if our previous definitions were applied without change. We shall first examine a permanent ITC, introducing some new definitions. After a comparative statics analysis, we then study the effects of a temporary ITC.

Permanent Investment Tax Credit

Recall that q is defined as the ratio of the market value of newly installed capital goods to their uninstalled cost. Up to this point we have included the ITC in the numerator and have set the denominator equal to one, the price of output. A more convenient, but equivalent, formulation for the study of the ITC is to subtract the ITC from the denominator of q rather than including it in the numerator. That is, the ITC is viewed as an immediate rebate which reduces the purchase price of new capital goods, rather than being capitalized into the value of an asset. We define q^*_t as the market value of capital goods, ignoring the ITC. Consistent with this definition, $q_t = q^*_t/(1-k)$. Assuming that output is expected to remain at Q_o forever, we obtain the following expression for q^*_t:

$$\text{(VI.B.1)} \quad q^*_t = \int_t^\infty (1-\tau) \frac{1-\alpha}{\alpha} \bar{w}\left(\frac{Q_o}{AK_s}\right)^{1/\alpha} e^{-(r+\delta)(s-t)} ds + \tau z q^*_t$$

or

$$q^*_t = \frac{1-\tau}{1-\tau z} \frac{1-\alpha}{\alpha} \bar{w} \int_t^\infty \left(\frac{Q_o}{AK_s}\right)^{1/\alpha} e^{-(r+\delta)(s-t)} ds$$

We divide q^*_t by 1-k to obtain an expression for q_t

$$\text{(VI.B.2)} \quad q_t = \frac{1-\tau}{(1-k)(1-\tau z)} \frac{1-\alpha}{\alpha} \bar{w} \int_t^\infty \left(\frac{Q_o}{AK_s}\right)^{1/\alpha} e^{-(r+\delta)(s-t)} ds$$

Note that this expression is the same as (III.4). Differentiating (VI.B.1) and (VI.B.2) with respect to time we obtain the equations of motion for q^*_t and q_t.

$$\text{(VI.B.3)} \quad \dot{q}^*_t = \frac{-(1-\tau)}{1-\tau z} \frac{1-\alpha}{\alpha} \bar{w} \left(\frac{Q_o}{AK_t}\right)^{1/\alpha} + (r+\delta) q^*_t$$

$$\text{(VI.B.4)} \quad \dot{q}_t = \frac{-(1-\tau)}{(1-k)(1-\tau z)} \frac{1-\alpha}{\alpha} \bar{w} \left(\frac{Q_o}{AK_t}\right)^{1/\alpha} + (r+\delta) q_t$$

Figure VI.B.1 presents stable paths to long-run equilibrium for k = 0, i.e., for zero ITC, and for k = k'. Note that the $\dot{q} = 0$ locus for k = k' is 1/(1-k') times as high as the $\dot{q} = 0$ locus for k = 0. In the absence of an ITC, the long-run capital stock is K_o and the long-run value of q is $\bar{q}_o$. Under a permanent ITC, the long-run equilibrium is at E_1,

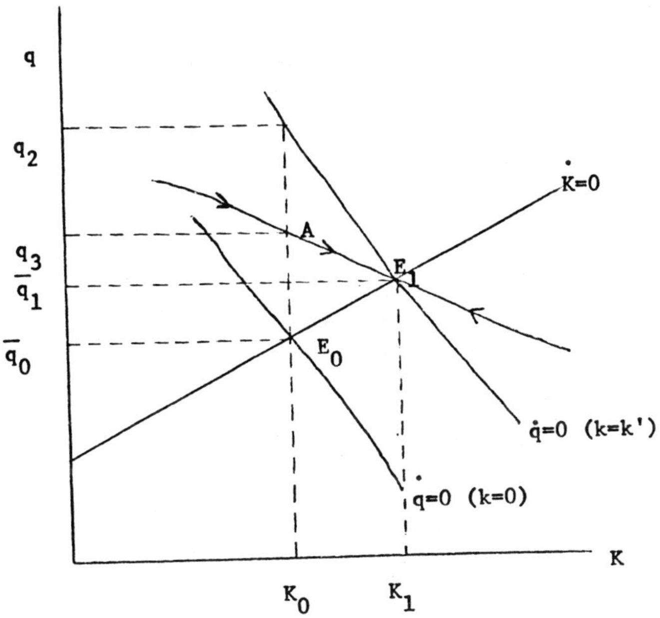

Figure VI.B.1

with a higher capital stock than at E_o. In order to maintain the higher capital stock in the face of depreciation, a higher long-run level of q is required to induce the necessary gross investment. Note, however, that the market value of capital q^*_t is lower at E_1 than at E_o. In long-run equilibrium, the higher level of the capital stock implies that the marginal rate of substitution of labor for capital is smaller and hence that the market value of capital goods is lower than at E_o. This may be illustrated in terms of figure IV.B.1 by noting that $\bar{q}_1 < q_2 = \bar{q}_o/(1-k')$. Therefore, the market value of capital with an ITC, at E_1, $(1-k')\bar{q}_1$, is less than $\bar{q}_o$, the market value of capital in the absence of an ITC at E_o. Also note that starting from initial long-run equilibrium at E_o, q jumps immediately to A. However, since q_3 is less than q_2, the market value of capital, q^*_t, falls immediately. At each future time period the capital stock will be higher than previously anticipated thus causing a reduction in q^*_t.

Temporary Investment Tax Credit

A temporary ITC is generally believed to have a more stimulative effect on current investment because it induces an intertemporal shifting of investment expenditures toward the present and near-future in order to take advantage of the ITC while it is available. As for long-run effects, it is clear that a temporary ITC cannot affect the steady state (as long as it is possible for $\dot{K}$ to be negative).

The analysis of a temporary ITC combines an analysis of anticipated and unanticipated changes. We shall assume that today, time t_o, it is unexpectedly announced that an ITC will go into effect immediately and that it will be removed at time t_1 in the future. The stable path corresponding to zero ITC passes through E_o and the stable path corresponding to a permanent ITC of k' passes through E_1. The dashed line through E_2 is 1/(1-k') as high as the stable path through E_o. Suppose we are initially at A and that an ITC is announced, effective immediately. If the ITC lasts only instantaneously, there is an immediate jump to B and then an immediate return to A. The effect of the ITC is then to cause an instantaneous jump in the rate

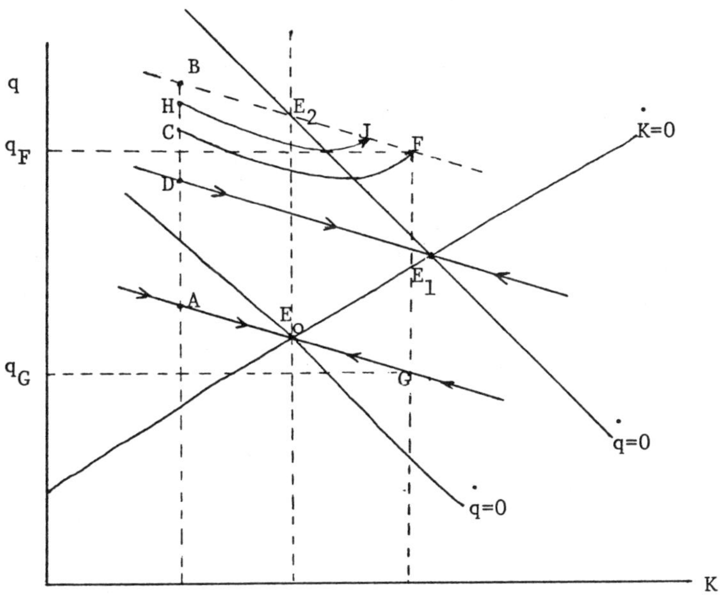

Figure VI.B.2

of investment to the higher (but still finite) level corresponding to point B. Since the ITC is in effect for only an infinitesimal time interval, the path of the capital stock is unaffected relative to what would have occurred without the ITC. Thus the market value q^*_t never departs from the stable path through E_o. Now, the polar opposite case is an ITC which lasts forever. As in the previous subsection, q jumps immediately to its value at D and the system proceeds along the stable path to E_1. The market value q^*_t falls immediately because the higher future path of the capital stock reduces the marginal value of capital at all future times.

Now we are ready to study the intermediate case which is of greatest interest. If the ITC is expected to remain in effect until time t_1, q_t jumps immediately to C and then proceeds to F as shown by the arrow. At time t_1, the system is at F, and when the ITC is removed, the system jumps instantaneously to G. Then the system proceeds smoothly to the long-run equilibrium at E_o. Note that for this particular case, neither q_t nor K_t moves monotonically to long-run equilibrium at E_o. Indeed, q_t does not even move continuously to long-run equilibrium, even after the initial unexpected jump.

The behavior of q_t over time deserves further comment. As in previous examples, there is an immediate (unanticipated) jump in q_t. However, there is a second discontinuous break in the path of q_t at time t_1, when the ITC is removed. At first glance, this might appear to violate the requirement that there be no anticipated windfall capital gains or losses. However, it is not the ratio q_t which is required to move continuously throughout the future. Rather, it is the numerator of q_t, i.e., the market value, q^*_t, which cannot have any anticipated discontinuous movements. (However, even q^*_t has an <u>unanticipated</u> immediate drop when the ITC is announced.) While it is true that q_t is anticipated to fall discontinuously from q_F to q_G, q^*_t does not jump discontinuously since $q_F(1-k') = q_G$. Therefore, the anticipated discontinuity in q_t does not reflect some sort of market failure. The discontinuity does imply that there will be a discontinuous decline in the rate of investment at time t_1. This discontinuity in the rate of investment seems quite reasonable since the ITC is a reward to the act of investment, not to capital *per se*. When the reward to investment stops abruptly, the rate of investment falls by a quantum amount.

The size of the jump in q_t and the fall in q^*_t when a temporary ITC is unexpectedly announced is related to the length of time for which the ITC is expected to last. In Figure VI.B.2, path HJ represents the path of the system corresponding to a more short-lived ITC than that represented by CF. The shorter ITC induces a larger jump in q_t and hence a smaller drop in q^*_t. Therefore, the rate of investment rises more sharply.

We have shown above that the announcement of an ITC caused a discrete fall in q^*_t, the market value of capital. It should not be inferred from the drop in q^*_t that the market value of firms drops by a discrete amount. Although the marginal value of capital falls, the owners of the firm's equity have a claim on the rents of the firm as well as the returns to the firm's capital. We shall show that the market value of the firm increases when the ITC is announced, despite the fact that q^*_t falls. We define the market value of the firm as the present discounted value of the future net cash flow produced by the firm. Assuming output to remain at Q_o forever, and that there is no ITC, now or in the future, the market value of the firm, as a function of the path of future investment $\{I\}$, is given by

$$\text{(VI.B.5)}\quad V_o(\{I\}) = \int_0^\infty \{ (Q_o - \bar{w}\,(\frac{Q_o}{A})^{1/\alpha} K_t^{1-\frac{1}{\alpha}})(1-\tau) - (1-\tau z)(I+c(I)) \} e^{-rt} dt$$

We shall assume that the managers of the firm choose $\{I\}$ so as to maximize $V_o(\{I\})$. Let $\{I^*\}$ be the path of investment which maximizes

$V_o(\{I\})$ so that the market value is $V_o(\{I^*\})$. Now assume that an ITC unexpectedly goes into effect today and will be removed at time t'. The managers of the firm will now try to maximize

$$(\text{VI.B.6}) \quad V_1(\{I\}) = \int_0^{t'} \{(Q_o - \bar{w}(\frac{Q_o}{A})^{\frac{1}{\alpha}} K_t^{1-\frac{1}{\alpha}})(1-\tau) - (1-k)(1-\tau z)(I+c(I))\}e^{-rt}dt$$

$$+ \int_{t'}^{\infty} \{(Q_o - \bar{w}(\frac{Q_o}{A})^{\frac{1}{\alpha}} K_t^{1-\frac{1}{\alpha}})(1-\tau) - (1-\tau z)(I + c(I))\}e^{-rt}dt.$$

Note that the path of investment $\{I^*\}$ is still feasible so that the new market value of the firm is at least $V_1(\{I^*\})$. But from (VI.B.5) and (V.B.6), it is clear that

$$(\text{VI.B.7}) \quad V_1(\{I^*\}) = V_o(\{I^*\}) + k(1-\tau z)\int_0^{t'} (I^* + c(I^*))e^{-rt}dt$$

As long as gross investment is never negative (which is a reasonable constraint to impose on the maximization problem), $V_1(\{I^*\}) \geq V_o(\{I^*\})$. Since the maximum of $V_1(\{I\})$ cannot be less than $V_1(\{I^*\})$, it is clear that the market value of the firm cannot decline when an ITC is announced.

In this subsection we have shown that any increase in the ITC, whether temporary or permanent, increases the market value of firms. As far as today's rate of investment is concerned, the shorter the duration of the ITC, the larger will be the increase in the rate of investment. Hence, explicitly temporary changes in the ITC may provide an effective tool for short-run macroeconomic policy.

VII. A Reinterpretation of the Empirical Implications of the Putty-Clay Hypothesis

The major empirical implication of the putty-clay hypothesis is that investment responds more rapidly to an increase in expected output than to an equivalent decrease in the cost of capital.[1] However, we demonstrate in this section that the same relative dynamic paths may be derived from the putty-putty model of this paper.[2] For simplicity, the analysis of this section uses a stripped-down version of our model. We ignore all taxes, assume that output is to remain constant and assume that the total installation cost during time interval dt is c(I)dt. Then from (V.4), we obtain

$$\text{(VII.1)} \quad \dot{P}_K = (r+\delta)P_K - \frac{1-\alpha}{\alpha}\bar{w} \left(\frac{\bar{Q}}{AK}\right)^{1/\alpha} .$$

Clearly, the $\dot{P}_K = 0$ locus is downward sloping in (K,P_K) space. The second equation of motion is $\dot{K} = I(P_K) - \delta K$. Recall that the $\dot{K} = 0$ locus slopes upward in (K,P_K) space.

Suppose we are initially in steady state equilibrium at E_o in figure (VII.1). Now consider two changes which have identical effects in the steady state.

Case I Consider a decrease in the discount rate by Δr. Now we obtain

$$\text{(VII.2)} \quad \dot{P}_K^I = (r - \Delta r + \delta)P_K - \frac{1-\alpha}{\alpha} w \left(\frac{\bar{Q}}{AK}\right)^{1/\alpha}$$

where the superscript I indicates that we are considering case I. This

---

[1]See Bischoff (1971)

[2]By"putty-putty" we mean that the production function is characterized by equal ex post and ex ante factor substitutability.

decrease in r shifts the $\dot{P}_K = 0$ locus upward so that it intersects the $\dot{K} = 0$ locus at E_1. The new steady state is characterized by a higher level of K and a higher rate of replacement investment to maintain the level of the capital stock.

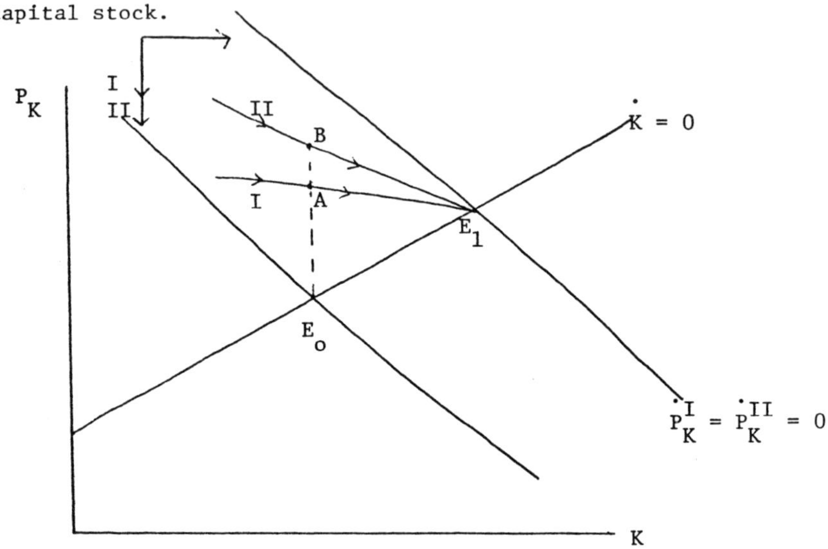

Figure VII.1

Case II Now consider an increase in output by the factor $\left(\frac{r+\delta}{r-\Delta r+\delta}\right)^{\alpha}$

We readily obtain

$$\text{(VII.3)} \quad \dot{P}_K^{II} = (r+\delta)P_K - \frac{1-\alpha}{\alpha} w \frac{r+\delta}{r-\Delta r+\delta}\left(\frac{\overline{Q}}{AK}\right)^{1/\alpha}$$

$$= \frac{r+\delta}{r-\Delta r+\delta}\left((r-\Delta r+\delta)P_K - \frac{1-\alpha}{\alpha} w \left(\frac{\overline{Q}}{AK}\right)^{1/\alpha}\right)$$

Combining (VII.2) and (VII.3) we obtain

$$\text{(VII.4)} \quad \dot{P}_K^{II} = \frac{r+\delta}{r-\Delta r+\delta} \dot{P}_K^{I} .$$

Since $\frac{r+\delta}{r-\Delta r+\delta} > 1$, we note that $|\dot{P}_K^{II}| > |\dot{P}_K^{I}|$ and that $\dot{P}_K^{II} = 0$ when and only when $\dot{P}_K^{I} = 0$. Thus the $\dot{P}_K^{II} = 0$ locus coincides with the $\dot{P}_K^{I} = 0$ locus so that the steady state is the same in case I and in case II. Note that we have drawn the vectors of motion to the northwest of E_1. At any point in (K,P_K) space, $\dot{K}$, represented by the horizontal arrow, is the same in both cases. However, the downward pointing arrow for $\dot{P}_K$ is longer in case II than in case I. Thus the stable path to equilibrium is steeper in case II than in case I. In case I, the system jumps to A when the unanticipated decrease in the discount factor occurs. In case II, the system jumps to B when the unanticipated increase in output occurs. Since the rate of investment is higher at B than at A, we get the putty-clay implication of a sharper response of investment to an increase in expected output than to an equivalent decrease in the discount rate. That is, we have derived a so-called putty-clay implication from a putty-putty model. This result is not a refutation of the putty-clay hypothesis. Rather the result is a warning that the empirical finding of a longer distributed lag response to cost of capital decreases than to output increases cannot necessarily be taken as proof of the putty-clay hypothesis.

VIII. Concluding Remarks

This paper has integrated two major theories of investment while taking explicit account of adjustment costs. The rate of investment is determined by q with the functional form of the relationship depending on adjustment costs. We have shown that q depends on technology, the real wage rate, the discount rate, the rate of growth of output, the corporate tax rate, depreciation allowance, physical depreciation, investment tax credit, and the stock of capital. The q approach was shown to yield many results which are similar to those derived from the standard neoclassical model. However, the q approach allows for a much richer analysis of dynamics. To study the dynamic effects of policy, this paper has borrowed the tax policy analysis of the standard neoclassical approach and has incorporated it into the q approach. Finally, this paper has raised an interesting challenge to the empirical evidence supporting the putty-clay hypothesis by showing that the so-called putty-clay implications for dynamic responses to exogenous shocks are consistent with a putty-putty model.

The analysis of this paper can be extended in two directions. The theoretical analysis can be extended by examining investment in a general equilibrium framework. As for empirical work, there seems to be a real need for investment functions which are free from the *ad hoc* distributed lags used in the estimation of standard neoclassical investment demand functions. Adjustment costs also warrant further study, both theoretically and empirically.

ESSAY II

INVESTMENT, q, AND RATIONAL EXPECTATIONS

I. Introduction

It has been argued by Tobin[1] and others that the rate of aggregate investment is an increasing function of q, where q is defined as the ratio of the market value of installed capital to the cost of uninstalled capital goods. Whereas previous empirical work (Ciccolo, 1975) has used the market value of the firm, as measured by stock market valuation, to construct a series for q, I have derived a formula for q based on the production function, the tax structure, the predicted path of output and future wage rates (see Abel, April 1977). Although the stock market valuation incorporates all of this information as well as any other relevant information, the stock market values the firm, not the firm's productive capital. These two values generally move together but there are important cases in which they move in opposite directions. For example, as was shown in my previous work, the enactment of an investment tax credit would increase the market value of the firm but would reduce the market value of capital, at the margin. Since it is the value of capital which is the appropriate numerator of q, I have departed from the practice of using stock market valuation to determine q.[2] Although the series of q values which I employ may be theoretically superior to stock market

---

[1] See Tobin (1961) for an early discussion of the concept of q. This crucial variable is actually named q in Brainard and Tobin (1968)).

[2] Note, however, that in this case the denominator of q falls more than the numerator so that q, and *a fortiori* investment, rises.

values in some respects, there are some shortcomings. My valuation formula ignores the effects of diversification on valuation. However, since I am dealing with an aggregate production function in a one-sector economy, the simple pre-portfolio theoretic valuation approach seems reasonable. A more important shortcoming of my approach relative to the stock market valuation approach is that I must deal explicitly with expectations formation, rather than rely on an efficient market to calculate expectations and properly incorporate them into the value of capital. This paper assumes that there are rational expectations with respect to the future rental value of capital and explores the implications of rational expectations for the estimation of forward-looking structural equations. An estimation procedure for infinite geometrically declining distributed leads on uncertain variables is developed. A major advantage of the approach of this paper is that by using a series for q based on the production function, the tax structure and future outputs and wage rates, we can examine the determinants of the market value of capital. In a sense, the approach of this paper is more structural than merely observing stock market values. For the purpose of policy evaluation, it is much more useful to have a structural model than to base predictions on guesses about stock and bond values.

Section II presents a brief derivation of the expression for q which will be used in this paper. In Section III, we construct a series for the rental value of capital services and examine the implied q series. An estimation technique for equations with an infinite distributed lead on the rational expectations of future variables is developed in Section IV. This procedure is applied in

Section V to estimate an aggregate investment equation. Concluding remarks are presented in Section VI.

II. The Derivation of q

The variable q is defined as the ratio of the market value of installed capital to the purchase price of uninstalled capital goods. In this section, we develop an expression for q based on the production function, the tax structure, and future wage rates and output levels. The derivation presented in this section is brief; a more complete discussion may be found in Essay I. For the sake of expositional simplicity, we assume that there is perfect foresight with respect to future output and wage levels so that we do not have to deal explicitly with uncertainty in this section. The discussion of uncertainty and expectational errors is postponed until Section IV when we discuss the econometrics of distributed leads on rational expectations of future variables.

Suppose that we are currently at time t, formulating the investment plans for the present and future. Assume that we know the path of future output X_s, $s \geq t$, and future wage rates w_s, $s \geq t$. Finally, assume that there is a neoclassical putty-putty production function with capital and labor as inputs, i.e., there are smoothly continuous substitution possibilities between capital, K_s, and labor, L_s, even after the capital is in place. An additional unit of capital at time s would allow the output level X_s to be produced with MRS_s fewer units of labor, where MRS_s is the marginal rate of substitution of labor for capital at time s. The consequent wage bill saving is thus $w_s \cdot MRS_s$. If an additional unit of capital is installed today, at time t, and if δ is the rate of physical depreciation, then at time s, only $e^{-\delta(s-t)}$ units of that capital remain. Hence, the pre-tax wage bill saving at time s, accruing to a unit of capital installed at time t, is $w_s \cdot MRS_s e^{-\delta(s-t)}$. Let τ_s be the rate of corporate taxation at time s, so that after-tax wage bill saving at time s is $(1-\tau_s)w_s MRS_s e^{-\delta(s-t)}$. Assuming that the discount rate is r, the present value of the stream of after-tax wage bill savings accruing to a unit of capital installed at time t is

$$\text{(II.1)} \qquad \text{market value} = \int_t^\infty (1-\tau_s)w_s \cdot MRS_s e^{-(r+\delta)(s-t)} ds \ .$$

This is the numerator of q. However, this derivation has ignored two aspects of the tax code which increase the market value of capital above the value given in (II.1).

First we consider the investment tax credit. Let k_t be the rate of investment tax credit at time t. If the firm is allowed to capitalize installation costs, so that the investment tax credit is based on the purchase price of uninstalled capital goods plus the installation costs, then the tax saving at time t is $k_t V_t$ where V_t is the market value of installed capital goods.[1] The second aspect of the tax code which tends to increase the market value of capital is the depreciation allowance. Let D(x) be the fraction of the depreciation base which may be deducted as an expense when a unit of capital

[1] It was shown in Essay I that the market value of installed capital goods is equal to the purchase price of capital goods plus the costs of installation, at the margin.

has age x. Then if the depreciation base is V_t, the present value of the depreciation allowance is

$$V_t \int_t^{\infty} \tau_s D(s-t) e^{-r(s-t)} ds.$$

Define the variable d_t to be

$$d_t = \int_0^{\infty} D(x) e^{-rx} dx$$

so that the present value of the depreciation allowance is $V_t \tau_t d_t$. Note that we have assumed that the corporate tax rate, τ, remains constant for the depreciable life of the capital.[1] The value $V_t \tau_t d_t$ for the present value of the depreciation allowance is based on the fact that the depreciation base is the market value of capital V_t. However, under the Long Amendment, which was repealed in 1964, the depreciation base must be reduced by the amount of the investment tax credit, so that the present value of the depreciation allowance is $V_t(1-k_t)\tau_t d_t$.

Now combine expression (II.1) with the value of the investment tax credit $k_t V_t$ and the value of the depreciation allowance $V_t \tau_t d_t$ (or $(1-k_t)V_t \tau_t d_t$ under the Long Amendment) to obtain the market value of installed capital.

---

[1] This is inconsistent with the formulation in (II.1) where the corporate tax rate is allowed to vary over the future. The simplification in this paragraph allows us to use an available series for d_t. The effects of this simplification should be negligible.

$$\text{(II.2)} \quad \text{a.} \quad V_t = \int_t^{\infty} (1-\tau_s)w_s \cdot MRS_s e^{-(r+\delta)(s-t)} ds + k_t V_t + \tau_t d_t V_t$$

after the repeal of the Long Amendment; and

$$\text{b.} \quad V_t = \int_t^{\infty} (1-\tau_s)w_s \cdot MRS_s e^{-(r+\delta)(s-t)} ds + k_t V_t + (1-k_t)\tau_t d_t V_t$$

under the Long Amendment.

The value of q_t is now simply V_t/PK_t where PK_t is the price of uninstalled capital goods. In order to simplify the exposition later in the paper, we define

$$\text{(II.3)} \quad x_s = (1-\tau_s)w_s \cdot MRS_s ,$$

that is, x_s is the value of after-tax wage bill savings accruing to the marginal unit of capital at time s. Also define

$$\text{(II.4)} \quad \text{a.} \quad z_t = (1-k_t-\tau_t d_t) \cdot PK_t, \text{ after repeal of the Long Amendment;}$$

$$\text{and} \quad \text{b.} \quad z_t = (1-k_t)(1-\tau_t d_t) \cdot PK_t, \text{ under the Long Amendment.}$$

Hence, rearranging (II.2) and using the definitions (II.3) and (II.4), we obtain

$$\text{(II.5)} \quad q_t = \frac{1}{z_t} \int_t^{\infty} x_s e^{-(r+\delta)(s-t)} ds .$$

In the next section we discuss the empirical construction of x_s and z_t and examine the implied values for q_t.

III. Empirical Construction of q

In section II we derived a formula, (II.5), for q_t, based on the continuous time discounting of the after-tax cash flow accruing to an additional unit of capital. The discrete time analogue of (II.5) is

$$\text{(III.1)} \qquad q_t = \frac{1}{z_t} \sum_{s=0}^{\infty} x_{t+s} \frac{1}{(1+r+\delta)^s}$$

In this section we discuss the empirical construction of the components of q_t, namely x_t and z_t, for the private, domestic, nonfarm business sector. This data is taken largely from the data bank of the MPS model and is described more fully in the appendix. Note that the capital stock is an aggregate of producers' structures and producers' durables. Where different values of the tax parameters or prices apply for structures and durables, a weighted average of the appropriate series is used.

Construction of x_t

Recall from (II.3) that x_t is defined as the after-tax wage bill saving accruing to the marginal unit of capital at time t, i.e., $x_t = (1-\tau_t)w_t \cdot MRS_t$. The corporate tax rate τ_t is the marginal tax rate applicable to earnings in the highest bracket. The wage rate w_t is the employee compensation rate in the private domestic nonfarm business sector. The marginal rate of substitution, MRS_t, is calculated from the production function. Assume that there is an aggregate Cobb-Douglas production function with a constant rate of technical progress g so that

$$\text{(III.2)} \quad X_t = AL_t^{\alpha}K_t^{1-\alpha}e^{gt} .$$

The marginal rate of substitution of labor for capital is easily derived to be

$$\text{(III.3)} \quad \text{a.} \quad MRS_t = \frac{1-\alpha}{\alpha} \frac{L_t}{K_t}$$

$$\text{b.} \quad = \frac{1-\alpha}{\alpha} \left(\frac{X_t}{AK_t}\right)^{1/\alpha} e^{-(1/\alpha)gt}$$

The expression for MRS_t given by (III.3.a) is probably a better measure on theoretical grounds because it depends on fewer estimated parameters than does (III.3b), and it will be correct up to a multiplicative constant even if the parameter α is calculated incorrectly. However, this superiority depends on L_t being measured accurately. In the absence of any reason to believe that L_t is measured either more accurately or less accurately than X_t, we cannot determine which series is better. Therefore, both series are used.

When the production function (III.2) is written in log-log form, it is linear in the three parameters: ln A, α, and g. However, unconstrained estimation of these three parameters does not yield reasonable results in that the estimated value of α was not in a reasonable range around $2/3$ to $3/4$. However, if labor is paid the value of its marginal product, the parameter α is equal to the labor share of income. Over the sample of quarterly observations from 1948-I to 1976-IV, the average labor share was .6709 with a standard deviation of only .0111. Hence, we estimated (III.2) in log-log form constraining α to .6709. The estimated production function, using the iterated Cochrane-Orcutt technique, is[1]

$$\ln(X_t/K_t) = \underset{(.0379)}{1.1000} + \underset{\text{(constrained value)}}{.6709} \ln(L_t/K_t) + \underset{(.00045)}{.00324}\, t \tag{III.4}$$

$R^2 = .9940$ rho = .9383 D-W = 1.5860 Std error of regression (SER) = .0099

Note that the estimated rate of technical progress is a reasonable 1.3% per year. If this progress is entirely labor-augmenting, then the rate of labor augmentation is 1.9% per year.

The parameter estimates in (III.4) are used in conjunction with equations (III.3) to calculate two series for MRS_t. The means of the calculated MRS_t series are .1047 and .1028 using (III.3a) and (III.3b) respectively, and the correlation coefficient of the two series is .98. Thus the two series are quite similar, as expected.

---

[1] Despite the high degree of serial correlation, these parameter estimates are quite similar to those obtained by OLS. The production function as estimated by OLS is $\ln(X_t/K_t) = \underset{(.0058)}{1.0599} + \underset{\text{(constrained value)}}{.6709} \ln(L_t/K_t) + \underset{(.00008)}{.00373}\, t$.

Note that the 95% confidence interval for each of the estimated parameters in (III.4) contains the corresponding OLS parameter estimate. This is comforting since both sets of estimates are unbiased if L_t and K_t are exogenous, as assumed.

The MRS_t series can now be combined with the corporate tax rate and wage rate data to construct a series for $x_t = (1-\tau_t)w_t MRS_t$. The mean value of x_t over the sample 16.59 using (III.3a) or 16.41 using (III.3b). The respective standard deviations are 3.72 and 3.87.[1]

Construction of z_t

Recall from (II.4) that the calculation z_t requires the price of capital PK_t and the following tax parameters: k_t, the rate of investment tax credit; τ_t, the rate of corporate taxation; and d_t, the present value of the depreciation allowance. Note that for PK_t, k_t, and d_t, different values are given for durables and structures. A weighted average, with weights equaling the shares in the capital stock, is used for each of these variables. The mean value of z over the sample is 49.92 dollars per unit of capital, with a standard deviation of 16.35.

The Implied Value of q

The series of x_t and z_t along with a discount factor $1/(1+r+\delta)$ imply a series of values for q_t as given by the expression in (III.1).

---

[1] The marginal rate of substitution is expressed in units of labor per year per unit of capital so that x_t, the after-tax wage bill saving, is in terms of dollars per year per unit of capital. Since the unit of time in our data is 3 months, rather than a year, we must divide MRS_t and x_t by 4.0 to express them in terms of quarterly labor saving and quarterly wage bill saving per unit of capital.

Rather than try to calculate a long sum to approximate the expression for q_t in (III.1), we calculate a hypothetical, but presumably representative, value for q_t. We let z_t take on its mean value and assume that x_s remains at its mean value forever. Under these assumptions, we obtain

$$\text{(III.5)} \qquad q_t = \frac{1}{\bar{z}_t} \sum_{s=0}^{\infty} x_{t+s} \left(\frac{1}{1+r+\delta}\right)^s = \frac{\bar{x}}{\bar{z}} \left(1 + \frac{1}{r+\delta}\right)$$

where $\bar{x}$ and $\bar{z}$ denote the sample means of x_t and z_t respectively. As explained in footnote 6 above, we must divide $\bar{x}$ by 4.0 since the MRS is measured at annual rates and we are discounting over quarters rather than over years. Hence, we obtain

$$\text{(III.6)} \qquad q_t = \frac{16.41/4.0}{49.92} \left(1 + \frac{1}{r+\delta}\right) = .0822 \left(1 + \frac{1}{r+\delta}\right)$$

Now, to calculate the value for q_t we need the discount rate r and the rate of physical depreciation δ, expressed as quarterly rates. The average value of δ over the sample period is approximately 10% per year and a reasonable after-tax discount rate is 10%.[1] Hence, at quarterly rates, $r+\delta$ is 5%, implying an average value for q_t of 1.73. In the sample the implied range of q is 1.27 to 2.17.[2]

---

[1] Hall and Jorgenson in Fromm, et al., pp.30-31, use a before-tax discount rate of 20% .

[2] Both x_t and z_t trend upward over time since each contains a nominal variable which trends upward over time. Therefore, the range of $x_t/\bar{z}$ would provide too wide a range for the implied value of q because much of the variation in in $x_t/\bar{z}$ is due simply to the growth of the nominal wage rate. Therefore, the implied range for q is based on the range of x_t/z_t over the sample.

The range of values for q_t calculated above seems somewhat high. There are several possible explanations for this seemingly upward bias in q. The future returns which are discounted are uncertain. Although the discount rate r incorporates a risk premium, it may be that the risk premium is much higher for more distant returns. In this case, our formula would tend to overstate q. A very rough correction for this uncertainty about distant returns would be to truncate the infinite sum in (III.1). Let N be the upper limit for the index s. If N = 20, then the value of q must be reduced by 35.9% The corresponding reductions for N = 30 and N = 40 are 22.0% and 13.5%, respectively. These calculations suggest that if future returns five or ten years out are so uncertain that they are essentially ignored, then an estimate of q_t based on a constant infinite stream of returns discounted at a constant rate may considerably overstate q.

A more reasonable explanation for the overvaluation of q may be that the capital share $(r+\delta)K_tPK_t$ is understated. Recall that the labor share in income is .6709 so that the pre-tax capital share in income is .3291. However, the average value of $(r^*+\delta)K_tPK_t/X\$_t$ is only .2304, where r* is the pre-tax discount rate assumed to be 20% per year, δ is the 10% annual rate of physical depreciation, and $X\$_t$ is nominal income in period t. Thus it appears that one or more of $r^*+\delta$, PK_t, or K_t is understated and should be increased. If $r^*+\delta$ is increased, then the capitalized value of the constant stream of returns is reduced. If K_t is increased, then MRS_t in each period is reduced, thus reducing q_t. Since PK_t is the denominator of q_t, if PK_t is increased, then q_t is decreased. As a rough correction for the undervaluation of $(r^{*}+\delta)PK_tK_t$, we might multiply q_t by .2304/.3291, which implies a mean value for q_t of 1.21. The implied range of q_t is .89 to 1.52.

In this section we have constructed series for x_t and z_t which are the building blocks of q_t. We then used these series to calculate hypothetical values for q_t as a rough check on the plausibility of the x_t and z_t series. It was found that x_t and z_t are of the right magnitude to imply values of q_t around 1.0 or slightly higher. Having verified that our data implies reasonable, or perhaps somewhat high, values for q_t, we now proceed to the econometric issues involved in estimating our investment function.[1]

IV. Rational Expectations and the Econometrics of Distributed Leads

It has been shown[2] that if the installation cost of capital goods is an increasing convex function of the ratio of gross investment to the capital stock, then I/K is an increasing function of q. We shall write the aggregate investment equation as

---

[1] Even if our data has a systematic tendency to overstate q_t, we may still obtain good estimates of the response of investment to q_t as long as the fluctuations in q_t are not distorted.

[2] See, among others, Essay I. This result is essentially contained in Treadway (1969) and in Gould (1968).

$$(IV.1) \qquad y_t = aq_t + b + e_t$$

where y_t is an increasing function of the investment capital ratio and the parameter a is positive by hypothesis. The first step in the estimation of (IV.1) would appear to be the construction of a series for q_t using the expression given in (III.1). However, there are several problems involved in constructing a series for q_t based on discounting future streams of returns over a long horizon. The choice of the length of the discounting horizon would be arbitrary and there is some question as to the appropriate rate of discount. Furthermore, a discounting horizon of any reasonable length would eat up degrees of freedom at the end of the sample. An additional problem arises because, in the presence of uncertainty, it is not certain *a priori* what future values should be discounted. Finally, a discounted sum over a long horizon simply may not exhibit enough movement to explain fluctuations in I/K. While these problems may not be insurmountable, we introduce an alternative method for the estimation of the investment equation. This alternative method has several advantages over the technique of constructing a q series from (III.1) and using the constructed q as a regressor in an investment equation. In the technique presented below, there is no arbitrary choice of the length of the discounting horizon and only the last observation of the sample must be sacrificed. In addition, this method provides an estimate of the discount factor $1/(1+r+\delta)$ which serves as a check on the plausibility of the results. Finally, this approach makes apparent the issues raised by rational expectations and expectational error and deals with them explicitly.

Let x^t_{t+k} be the expectation of x_{t+k} conditional on information available at the end of period t, and let $\gamma = 1/(1+r+\delta)$ be the constant discount factor applied to future returns. Then, if investors have certainty equivalence behavior, we may rewrite the expression for q_t in (III.1) as

$$\text{(IV.2)} \qquad q_t = \frac{1}{z_t}(x_t + \gamma x^t_{t+1} + \gamma^2 x^t_{t+2} + \ldots) ,$$

where we have used the fact that $x^t_t = x_t$. Now, substitute (IV.2) into (IV.1) to obtain

$$\text{(IV.3)} \qquad y_t = \frac{a}{z_t}(x_t + \gamma x^t_{t+1} + \gamma^2 x^t_{t+2} + \ldots) + b + e_t .$$

Equation (IV.3) is a distributed lead equation with geometrically declining weights; the similarity to the Koyck lag formulation is apparent. As with the standard geometrically declining lag formulation, direct estimation of (IV.3) would involve a loss of degrees of freedom and, if the nonlinear constraints on the parameters are not imposed, there will be severe multicollinearity. There are also important differences from the conventional geometrically declining lag formulation. In the case of lags, the constraint that the lags decline geometrically is often imposed only because of a feeling that the weights decline smoothly. In this particular application, the geometrically declining lead weights follow directly from the assumption of a constant rate of discount. A more important difference between leads and lags is that the expectations x^t_{t+k} are unobservable, even _ex post_. We discuss the problem of unobservable expectations below.

Rational Expectations

We deal with the problem of unobservable expectations directly by assuming that expectations are formed rationally. Let u^t_{t+k} be the error in the expectation of x_{t+k} formed at time t so that

$$(\text{IV.4}) \qquad x_{t+k} = x^t_{t+k} + u^t_{t+k}, \qquad k=1,2,3,\ldots$$

Rational expectations implies that $E_t(u^t_{t+k}) = 0$ for all t and k, where the subscript t indicates that the expectation is conditional on information available at the end of period t.

Now substitute (IV.4) into (IV.3) to obtain

$$(\text{IV.5}) \qquad y_t = \frac{a}{z_t}(x_t + \gamma x_{t+1} + \gamma^2 x_{t+2} + \ldots) - \frac{a}{z_t}(\gamma u^t_{t+1} + \gamma^2 u^t_{t+2} + \ldots) + b + e_t .$$

The first infinite sum on the right hand side involves only observables and estimable parameters. In order to reduce the number of observables which appear as regressors, we subtract $\gamma \frac{z_{t+1}}{z_t}$ from both sides of (IV.5) to obtain

$$(\text{IV.6}) \qquad y_t = \gamma \frac{z_{t+1}}{z_t} y_{t+1} + \frac{a}{z_t} x_t + b - b\gamma \frac{z_{t+1}}{z_t} -$$

$$- \frac{a}{z_t} \gamma u^{t}_{t+1} - \frac{a}{z_t} \sum_{k=2}^{\infty} (u^{t}_{t+k} - u^{t+1}_{t+k})\gamma^{k} + e_t - \gamma \frac{z_{t+1}}{z_t} e_{t+1}$$

Noting that $u^{t+1}_{t+1} = 0$, we may rewrite (IV.6) as (IV.7)

$$\text{(IV.7)} \qquad y_t = \gamma \frac{z_{t+1}}{z_t} y_{t+1} + \frac{a}{z_t} x_t + b - b\,\gamma \frac{z_{t+1}}{z_t}$$

$$- \frac{a}{z_t} \sum_{k=1}^{\infty} (u^{t}_{t+k} - u^{t+1}_{t+k})\gamma^{k} + e_t - \gamma \frac{z_{t+1}}{z_t} e_{t+1}.$$

The disturbance term contains an infinite sum of $(u^{t}_{t+k} - u^{t+1}_{t+k})\gamma^{k}$. To interpret this infinite sum, note from (IV.4) that

$$\text{(IV.8)} \qquad u^{t}_{t+k} - u^{t+1}_{t+k} = x^{t+1}_{t+k} - x^{t}_{t+k} .$$

That is, the change in the expectational error from period t to period t+1 is equal to the change in the expectation from period t to period t+1. This follows from the fact that in every period, the expectation of some future variable plus the expectational error, is equal to its subsequent realization. Combining (IV.7) and (IV.8), we obtain

$$\text{(IV.9)} \qquad y_t = \gamma \frac{z_{t+1}}{z_t} y_{t+1} + \frac{a}{z_t} x_t + b - b\,\gamma \frac{z_{t+1}}{z_t} - \frac{a}{z_t} R_{t+1} + e_t - \gamma \frac{z_{t+1}}{z_t} e_{t+1}$$

where $$R_{t+1} = \sum_{k=1}^{\infty} (x^{t+1}_{t+k} - x^{t}_{t+k})\gamma^{k} .$$

Note that the variable R_{t+1} is equal to the discounted value at the end of period t, of revisions in expectations about x_{t+k}, based on information which becomes available in period t+1. Since R_{t+1} is based on innovations in period t+1, it is correlated with y_{t+1} and hence OLS would yield inconsistent estimates of the parameters in (IV.9).

Before discussing consistent estimation of (IV.9), it may be useful to examine the economic intuition behind this equation. First consider variations in y_{t+1} and x_t for given z_t and z_{t+1}. The coefficient a should be positive since the higher is the first of a stream of returns, x_t, the higher is the discounted value of the entire stream of returns and hence the higher is the rate of investment. As for y_{t+1}, it may be high for two reasons. If a high value of y_{t+1} reflects optimistic expectations about future x_{t+k} as of time t and time t+1, then current investment, y_t, should be high. However, if y_{t+1} is large because expectations are revised upward in period t+1, then this should not be reflected in y_t. This is the role played by the discounted sum of revisions, R_{t+1}, in the disturbance term. It lowers y_t for given y_{t+1} if the high value of y_{t+1} is due to information which was not available before the beginning of period t+1.

We now examine the role of z_t and z_{t+1} holding x_t and y_{t+1} constant. Note that (IV.9) may be rewritten as

$$\text{(IV.10)} \quad y_t = \frac{a}{z_t} x_t + b + \gamma \frac{z_{t+1}}{z_t} (y_{t+1} - b - e_{t+1}) + e_t - \frac{a}{z_t} R_{t+1} ,$$

where the term in parentheses is positive.[1]

---

[1] $y_{t+1} - b - e_{t+1} = \frac{a}{z_{t+1}}(x_{t+1} + \gamma x^{t+1}_{t+2} + \gamma^2 x^{t+1}_{t+3} + \ldots)$ which is positive as long as a is positive.

Therefore, an increase in z_{t+1}/z_t would increase the current rate of investment y_t. Recall that z_t is essentially the price of uninstalled capital goods. An increase in z_{t+1}/z_t would correspond to a rise in capital goods prices in period t+1 and would induce an increase in the current purchase of capital goods.[1] Observe also that a decrease in the current price of uninstalled capital goods z_t would lead to an increase in the rate of investment.

The parameters a, b, and γ may be consistently estimated by an instrumental variable regression of y_t on x_t/z_t, $z_{t+1}y_{t+1}/z_t$, z_{t+1}/z_t, and a constant. If e_t is white noise and if x_t/z_t, z_{t+1}/z_t, and y_{t-1}/z_t are uncorrelated with the revisions in expectations, R_{t+1}, then valid instruments would be x_t/z_t, z_{t+1}/z_t, y_{t-1}/z_t, and a constant. It is important to use valid instruments, because as shown in Abel (September 1977), OLS can be very biased when the disturbance term contains the discounted value of revisions in expectations. In some cases, the estimates may be biased more than 100% toward zero, i.e., the bias may be so strong as to give the wrong sign to the estimated parameters, even asymptotically.

The need for instrumental variables generally arises because the disturbance term contains some omitted variable which is correlated with the regressors. If the omitted variable is not observable, either directly, or via proxy, then there is no alternative to instrumental variable estimation. However, if the omitted variable, or a reasonable proxy, can be included as a regressor, then the need for instruments is eliminated, or less burden is placed on the instru-

---

[1] We have implicitly assumed that the one-period inflation rate in z is known.

ments. In the estimation of (IV.9) recall that much of the problem with obtaining consistent estimates is due to the discounted value of revisions, R_{t+1}, which appears in the disturbance term and is correlated with y_{t+1}. Since all x^{t+1}_{t+k}, k=1,2,3,... are based on the same information set, the expectation x^{t+1}_{t+1} incorporates the new information upon which R_{t+1} is based. Recall that this particular expectation is observable since $x^{t+1}_{t+1} = x_{t+1}$. Therefore, it may be reasonable to use x_{t+1} to measure R_{t+1}, the discounted value of revisions which appears in the disturbance term. We examine this proposal more rigorously below.

The Revisions of Expectations

We now examine the role of x_{t+1} as a proxy for R_{t+1}, the discounted value of revisions in expectations. Suppose that x_t is generated by an autoregressive process (AR) of order m, where m may be infinite. Then x_t may be expressed as

$$\text{(IV.11)} \qquad x_t = \phi(L)x_t + n_t$$

where $\phi(L) = \sum_{i=1}^{m} \phi_i L^i$ is a lag polynomial of order m, and n_t is a white noise innovation. If expectations of x_t are formed rationally, it can be shown that the discounted value of revisions, R_{t+1}, in (IV.9) is[1]

---

[1] This formula is based on the assumption that the discounted value of revisions is finite. A necessary condition for the sum to be finite is that all roots of the characteristic equation $1 - \phi(\lambda) = 0$ have modulus greater than the discount factor γ. If this condition holds, then $1 - \phi(\gamma) > 0$. Observe that stationarity of x_t would imply that this condition holds since $|\gamma| < 1$ and all roots of $1 - \phi(\lambda) = 0$ lie outside the unit circle for a stationary process.

$$\text{(IV.12)} \qquad R_{t+1} = \frac{\gamma}{1-\phi(\gamma)} n_{t+1}$$

This formula is similar to the one given in Flavin (1977). However, the present application of this formula differs greatly from Flavin's approach. She actually estimates the innovation n_{t+1} as a residual from an estimated AR process and then uses the constructed series of innovations as a regressor in a life-cycle consumption function. In this paper, the estimation of the investment equation will not require prior estimation of an AR process and construction of a series of innovations. However, the interpretation of some parameters will require estimation of an AR process.

The innovation n_{t+1} is an unobservable variable which is reflected in x_{t+1} and subsequent x_{t+k}. Therefore, the expression for R_{t+1} in (IV.12) cannot be substituted directly into (IV.9) and used as a regressor. However, combining (IV.11) and (IV.12), we obtain an expression for R_{t+1} in terms of observables

$$\text{(IV.13)} \qquad R_{t+1} = \frac{\gamma}{1-\phi(\gamma)} (1 - \phi(L))x_{t+1} .$$

Note that $\left.\frac{dR_{t+1}}{dx_{t+1}}\right|_{x_t, x_{t-1}, \ldots} = \frac{\gamma}{1-\phi(\gamma)}$. The numerator of this deviation, γ, is clearly positive. As for the denominator, it will be positive, if as we assume, R_{t+1} is finite.[1] Therefore,

---

[1] See footnote 1 on preceding page.

$\frac{dR_{t+1}}{dx_{t+1}} > 0$ so that a high value of x_{t+1} is associated with a high value of R_{t+1}. Now we may substitute (IV.13) into (IV.9) to obtain

$$\text{(IV.14)} \quad y_t = \gamma \frac{z_{t+1}}{z_t} y_{t+1} + a \frac{x_t}{z_t} + b - b\gamma \frac{z_{t+1}}{z_t} - \frac{a}{z_t} \frac{\gamma(1-\phi(L))x_{t+1}}{1-\phi(\gamma)} + $$

$$+ e_t - \gamma \frac{z_{t+1}}{z_t} e_{t+1} .$$

Rearranging (IV.14), and defining $\phi^*(L) = \sum_{i=2}^{m} \phi_i L^i$, we obtain

$$\text{(IV.15)} \quad y_t = \gamma \frac{z_{t+1}}{z_t} y_{t+1} + a \frac{1-\phi^*(\gamma)}{1-\phi(\gamma)} \frac{x_t}{z_t} + b - b\gamma \frac{z_{t+1}}{z_t} - a \frac{\gamma}{1-\phi(\gamma)} \frac{x_{t+1}}{z_t} +$$

$$+ a \frac{\gamma\phi^*(L)}{1-\phi(\gamma)} \frac{x_{t+1}}{z_t} + e_t - \gamma \frac{z_{t+1}}{z_t} e_{t+1}$$

Equation (IV.15) contains five regressors including a constant. The coefficient of $\frac{z_{t+1}}{z_t} y_{t+1}$ is simply γ, the discount factor, which on quarterly data should be between 0.9 and 1.0. As for the coefficient of $\frac{x_t}{z_t}$, we would empirically expect $1-\phi^*(\gamma) = (1-\phi(\gamma)) + \phi_1\gamma$ to be positive, since as explained above, $1-\phi(\gamma)$ should be positive and we would expect ϕ_1 to be positive for most economic time series. Therefore, since a is hypothesized to be positive, we would expect the coefficient of x_t/z_t to be positive. As for the coefficient of $\frac{x_{t+1}}{z_t}$, its expected sign is negative. The coefficients of $\frac{x_t}{z_t}$ and of $\frac{x_{t+1}}{z_t}$ should be of opposite sign and in the ratio $\frac{1-\phi^*(\gamma)}{\gamma}$. There is little _a priori_ knowledge about the constant b or about the coefficient of $\frac{z_{t+1}}{z_t}$ except that they have opposite signs and have magnitudes in the ratio of $1/\gamma$.

Before moving on to the estimation of the investment equation, observe that the disturbance term in (IV.13) contains $\phi^*(L)x_{t+1} = \sum_{i=2}^{m} \phi_i x_{t+1-i}$ which in general is correlated with x_t and x_{t+1}. If, however, x_t is generated by a first-order AR process, then $\phi^*(L)x_{t+1} \equiv 0$ and there is no problem. But if x_t is generated by an AR process of order two or higher, then $\phi^*(L)x_{t+1}$ is no longer identically zero, and correlation between the regressors and this component of the disturbance will bias the parameter estimates, even asymptotically. We must find instruments which are correlated with x_t and x_{t+1} and yet are uncorrelated with $x_{t-1}, x_{t-2}, \ldots$. In most economic time series it is reasonable to expect the autocorrelation function to die out as it is evaluated at higher order lags. Thus future values of x would be more highly correlated with x_t and x_{t+1} than with $x_{t-1}, x_{t-2}, \ldots$ Thus future x's may be reasonable instruments. In practice, the coefficients of the lag polynomial of order 2 or higher may be small enough so that the inconsistency due to the correlation of x_t and x_{t+1} with $\phi^*(L)v_{t+1}$ may be small. The lesson to be learned is that while choosing valid instruments for y_{t+1} or other endogenous variables, we would not want to use lagged values of x_t, since these lagged values are components of the error term.

V. Estimation of the Investment Equation

In this section, we estimate and interpret the parameters of (IV.15). For convenience, we rewrite (IV.15) as

$$(V.1) \qquad y_t = \gamma \frac{z_{t+1}}{z_t} y_{t+1} + A \frac{x_t}{z_t} + B \frac{x_{t+1}}{z_t} + b - b\gamma \frac{z_{t+1}}{z_t} + e^*_t$$

where
$$A = \frac{a(1-\phi^*(\gamma))}{1-\phi(\gamma)}$$

$$B = \frac{-a\gamma}{1-\phi(\gamma)}$$

$$e^*_t = -B \frac{\phi^*(L)x_{t+1}}{z_t} + e_t - \gamma \frac{z_{t+1}}{z_t} e_{t+1} .$$

Recall from section IV that y_t is defined as an increasing function of the investment capital ratio, I_t/K_t. We let $y_t = \ln(I_t/K_t)$. Now we are prepared to determine reasonable values for the estimated parameters. To summarize the _a priori_ knowledge of parameter values from section IV, recall that γ is the quarterly discount factor $1/(1+r+\delta)$ and a reasonable range for γ is .9 to 1.0. Also recall from section IV that we expect $1-\phi^*(\gamma)$ and $1-\phi(\gamma)$ to be positive so that A should be positive and B should be negative. Furthermore, $A/B = \frac{1}{\gamma} - \sum_{i=2}^{m} \phi_i \gamma^{i-1}$. To determine a reasonable value for b, we must leave the realm of _a priori_ knowledge and examine the data. Rearrange (IV.1) to obtain

$$(V.2) \qquad b = \bar{y} - a\bar{q} - \bar{e} ,$$

where a bar over a variable indicates its mean value in the sample. Empirically, $\bar{y}$ is equal to -3.3 in our sample. Although q is not measured directly, it is certainly positive and $\bar{q}$ is probably close to 1.0. By assumption, a is positive and $\bar{e}$ is small. Hence, we expect b to be algebraically less than -3.3.

In order to interpret the estimated coefficients of the investment equation, we fit an autoregressive process to x_t by regressing x_t on its own lagged values, up to a fourth-order lag. The results are shown in Table I. The regressions reported in Table I do not include a constant term; in all cases the value for the constant fails to be significantly different from zero, at even the

Table I

x_t As An Autoregressive Process

Dependent Variable: x_t

x_{t-1}	x_{t-2}	x_{t-3}	x_{t-4}	R^2	D-W	Standard error of regression
1.0080 (.0026)	--	--	--	.9860	1.6306	.4610
1.1914 (.0931)	-.1849 (.0939)	--	--	.9864	2.0098	.4572
1.1849 (.0954)	-.1417 (.1473)	-.0370 (.0964)	--	.9863	1.9890	.4609
1.1880 (.0961)	-.1347 (.1488)	-.1098 (.1489)	.0632 (.0975)	.9863	1.9832	.4638

10% level.[1] In terms of the standard error of regression and in

[1] It is reasonable that these fitted AR processes do not include a constant term since x_t is a nonstationary process, and the interpretation of the constant would be strained. Presumably, the mean of x_t increases slowly over time and the upward drift in the mean of x_t is captured by including lagged x_t's as regressors.

terms of the significance of the estimated parameters, the estimated second-order AR process seems to fit the x_t series best.[1] The first-order autoregressive process appears to be too simple to fit the data well. The Durbin-Watson statistic, which is biased toward 2.0 indicates that there may be some residual serial correlation. As for the third and fourth-order autoregressive processes, they have nothing to recommend them over the second-order process since their fit is no better and the coefficients of x_{t-3} and x_{t-4} are not at all significant. Thus, if one process has to be chosen, it would be the second-order process. However, the choice among the AR(2), AR(3), or AR(4) process is not really crucial since these three estimated processes have essentially the same implications for the interpretation of the coefficients. In Table II below, we present the values of $|A/B| = \frac{1}{\gamma} - \sum_{i=2}^{m} \phi_i \gamma^{i-1}$ for various discount factors γ and AR(m) processes.

Table II

Values of $|A/B|$

γ	.85	.90	.95	1.0
AR(2)	1.33	1.28	1.23	1.18
AR(3)	1.32	1.27	1.22	1.18
AR(4)	1.33	1.28	1.23	1.18

[1] The reader may wonder why R^2 is not maximized in the fourth-order AR process which has the most estimated parameters. The reason is that R^2 is not strictly comparable across equations because the samples are of different length; for each additional lagged variable which appears as a regressor, the sample is shortened by one observation. Note that the standard error of regression is corrected for degrees of freedom. Hence, the standard error of regression is smaller for the AR(2) process than for the AR(3) or AR(4) processes because it has more degrees of freedom and essentially the same fit.

Note that for a given value of γ, $|A/B|$ varies almost negligibly across AR(m) processes for m = 2,3,4. From this table it appears that the value of $|A/B|$ should be in the range 1.18 to 1.33.

As a first step in the estimation of the investment equation, we estimate (V.1) by OLS to obtain

$$\text{(V.3)} \qquad y_t = \underset{(.049)}{.879} \frac{z_{t+1}}{z_t} y_{t+1} + \underset{(.316)}{2.110} \frac{x_t}{z_t} - \underset{(.275)}{2.162} \frac{x_{t+1}}{z_t} + \underset{(.151)}{3.460} \frac{z_{t+1}}{z_t} - \underset{(.181)}{3.844}$$

R^2 = .9232 Standard error of regression = .0248

These estimated parameters agree very well with our a priori knowledge. All coefficients have the correct sign and the magnitudes of the coefficients are in line with our a priori knowledge, except that the estimated value of the discount factor appears to be somewhat low. However, these estimates are inconsistent because y_{t+1} is correlated with e_{t+1} which appears in the disturbance term, and $\frac{x_t}{z_t}$ and $\frac{x_{t+1}}{z_t}$ are correlated to some extent with $\phi^*(L) \frac{x_{t+1}}{z_t}$, which is a component of the disturbance term.

Ignoring, for the moment, the inconsistency due to the correlation between $\frac{x_t}{z_t}$, $\frac{x_{t+1}}{z_t}$, and the disturbance, which contains $\phi^*(L)x_{t+1}/z_t$, we re-estimate (V.1) by instrumental variables to obtain[1]

$$\text{(V.4)} \qquad y_t = \underset{(.157)}{.937}\ \frac{z_{t+1}}{z_t}\, y_{t+1} + \underset{(.624)}{1.877}\ \frac{x_t}{z_t} - \underset{(.394)}{2.044}\ \frac{x_{t+1}}{z_t} + \underset{(.269)}{3.528}\ \frac{z_{t+1}}{z_t} - \underset{(.406)}{3.680}$$

$R^2 = .9210 \qquad$ D-W = 1.6514, $\qquad$ SER = .0248

The instrument list purposely excludes lagged values of x_t since these are likely to be more correlated with $\phi^*(L)x_{t+1}/z_t$ in the disturbance term than with y_{t+1} which is treated as the only endogenous right-hand side variable. The coefficient estimates differ only slightly from the OLS estimates. The estimated discount factor increases somewhat to a more reasonable .937 per quarter, but the standard error of this coefficient is fairly large so we should not make too much of the improved point estimate.

The parameter estimates in (V.4) have not corrected for possible inconsistency arising from correlation between $\frac{x_t}{z_t}$, $\frac{x_{t+1}}{z_t}$ and $\frac{\phi^*(L)x_{t+1}}{z_t}$. Note that $\frac{\phi^*(L)x_{t+1}}{z_t}$ is simply an omitted variable and its coefficient is $-B$, i.e., equal in magnitude but opposite in sign to the coefficient of $\frac{x_{t+1}}{z_t}$. If we could include $\phi^*(L)\frac{x_{t+1}}{z_t}$ as a right-

---

1 The list of instrument candidates is $\frac{x_t}{z_t}, \frac{x_{t+1}}{z_t}, \frac{z_{t+1}}{z_t}, \frac{z_t}{z_{t-1}}, \frac{x_{t+1}}{z_{t+1}}, \frac{x_{t+2}}{z_{t+1}}$, and a constant. Different instrument lists yield insignificantly different results. In some cases the point estimate of the discount factor exceeds 1, but never significantly so.

hand side variable, and thereby remove it from the disturbance, then $\frac{x_t}{z_t}$ and $\frac{x_{t+1}}{z_t}$ would be uncorrelated with the disturbance and would be valid instruments. As an approximation, we set $\phi^*(L)x_{t+1}$ equal to $\sum_{i=2}^{m} \phi_i^{(m)} x_{t+1-i}$, for m=2,3,4, where $\phi_i^{(m)}$ is the estimated value of ϕ_i for an AR(m) process, as reported in Table I. Imposing the constraint that the coefficient of $\phi^*(L)x_{t+1}$ is opposite in sign but equal in magnitude to the coefficient of $\frac{x_{t+1}}{z_t}$, and using the same instruments as for (V.4), we obtain

$$\text{(V.5)} \quad y_t = \underset{(.190)}{.826} \frac{z_{t+1}}{z_t} y_{t+1} + \underset{(.866)}{2.726} \frac{x_t}{z_t} - \underset{(.490)}{2.291} (1-\phi^*(L)) \frac{x_{t+1}}{z_t} + \underset{(.313)}{3.362} \frac{z_{t+1}}{z_t} - \underset{(.493)}{3.948}$$

$R^2 = .9088 \qquad$ D-W = 1.5770 $\qquad$ SER = .0266

assuming that x_t is an AR(2) process. The results obtained assuming that x_t is an AR(3) or an AR(4) process are not substantially different. The parameter estimates in (V.5) all square quite well with our a priori knowledge except that the estimated discount factor is too low. However, the standard error of estimated discount factor is large enough so that the 95% confidence interval includes our a priori range of values. We note in (V.6) below that changing the list of instrument candidates gives us a more reasonable point estimate of the discount factor without causing a statistically significant change in any of the coefficient estimates.[1]

$$\text{(V.6)} \qquad y_t = \underset{(.128)}{.907} \frac{z_{t+1}}{z_t} y_{t+1} + \underset{(.619)}{2.440} \frac{x_t}{z_t} - \underset{(.381)}{2.166} (1-\phi^*(L)) \frac{x_{t+1}}{z_t}$$

$$+ \underset{(.236)}{3.489} \frac{z_{t+1}}{z_t} - \underset{(.345)}{3.756}$$

$R^2 = .9103 \qquad$ D-W = 1.6391 $\qquad$ SER = .0264

In this equation, all five coefficients have the anticipated sign and are quite significantly different from zero. The estimated discount factor still appears low for quarterly data. Note that the constant term was hypothesized to be algebraically less than -3.3 and satisfies this hypothesis. As for the coefficients of $\frac{x_t}{z_t}$ and $\frac{x_{t+1}}{z_t}$, the ratio of their magnitudes should be about 1.28. In equation (V.6), this ratio is 1.13 with a standard error of .11 so that we cannot reject the hypothesis that the ratio of coefficient magnitudes is actually equal to 1.28. Also note that the coefficient of $\frac{z_{t+1}}{z_t}$ divided by the magnitude of the constant term should be equal to the discount factor. This ratio, as calculated from (V.6) is .93 with a standard error of .13 so that these coefficients satisfy our *a priori* expectations.

The spirit of equation (V.6) has some similarity to the approach used in Flavin (1977) in which she directly estimates the

---

[1] The instruments used in the calculation of (V.6) are $\frac{x_t}{z_t}$, $\frac{x_{t+1}}{z_t}$, $\frac{x_{t+2}}{z_{t+2}}$, $\frac{z_{t+1}}{z_1}$, and a constant. When these instruments are used to re-estimate (V.4), there is virtually no change in the estimates reported for (V.4).

innovation $n_{t+1} = (1-\phi(L))x_{t+1}$, in the context of a life-cycle consumption function. In this paper, we have recognized that the innovations may be expressed as a function of x_{t+1} and x_t (and possibly lagged x_t's). However, it is not necessary to know the parameters, or even the degree, of the AR process generating the x_t's, in order to know the expected signs of the coefficients of $\frac{x_t}{z_t}$ and $\frac{x_{t+1}}{z_t}$.[1] In order to reduce the possible inconsistency arising from the correlation of the regressors with $\phi^*(L)\frac{x_{t+1}}{z_t}$, we have added $\phi^*(L)\frac{x_{t+1}}{z_t}$ to the list of regressors, with the appropriate constraint. This procedure is tantamount to estimating an AR process for x_t and using the estimated residuals as proxies for the revisions.

To calculate the responsiveness of investment with respect to q, we must recover the parameter a either from A, the coefficient of $\frac{x_t}{z_t}$, or from B, the coefficient of $\frac{x_{t+1}}{z_t}$. From equation (V.1), we recall that A and B are defined so that $a = A\,\frac{1-\phi(\gamma)}{1-\phi^*(\gamma)}$ or $a = -B\,\frac{1-\phi(\gamma)}{\gamma}$. In the first two columns of Table III, we present the values of $A\,\frac{1-\phi(\gamma)}{1-\phi^*(\gamma)}$ and $-B\,\frac{1-\phi(\gamma)}{\gamma}$ implied by the coefficients in equations (V.4), (V.5), and (V.6), assuming that x_t follows a second-order autoregressive process. The implied values of a are not very different if x_t follows a third-order or a fourth-order AR process.[2] We note that there is a great deal of variation in the implied values of a across the rows of Table III. However, as will be shown below, these very different values of a do not reflect

---

[1] The only information we require about the AR process to determine the signs of the coefficients of x_t/z_t and x_{t+1}/z_t *a priori* is that $1-\phi(\gamma) > 0$ and $\phi_1 >$

[2] In the calculation of a, the coefficients A and B have been multiplied by 4. since the data for x_t is a series of quarterly observations expressed at annual rates.

wildly different implied elasticities of I_t/K_t with respect to q_t. Rather, the large variation in calculated a reflects the different discount factors used in retrieving a from the coefficients A and B.

Table III

Implied Values of a and the Elasticity of I/K with Respect to q

Equation number	$a_A=A\frac{1-\phi(\gamma)}{1-\phi^*(\gamma)}$	$a_B=-B\frac{1-\phi(\gamma)}{\gamma}$	$a_A\,\frac{\bar{x}/\bar{z}}{1-\gamma}$	$a_B\,\frac{\bar{x}/\bar{z}}{1-\gamma}$
(V.4)	.296	.400	.386	.522
(V.5)	1.374	1.575	.649	.744
(V.6)	.604	.681	.543	.602

The elasticity of I/K with respect to q is equal to $\frac{d\ \ln(I/K)}{dq}\cdot$ $q = a\cdot q$. If the mean value of q were in the vicinity of 1.0, then the parameter a would be an estimate of the elasticity evaluated at the mean. However, as pointed out in section III, q is not equal to 1.0 in our sample. The implied value of q in our sample is approximately $\frac{x_t/z_t}{1-\gamma}$ so that the elasticity evaluated at the mean is $a\,\frac{\bar{x}}{\bar{z}(1-\gamma)}$. Using this expression, estimates of the elasticity of I/K with respect to q, derived from the coefficients A and B, are presented in columns 3 and 4 of Table III. Note that there is not nearly as much variation in the calculated elasticities as in the calculated values of a. As explained earlier, the parameter estimates in (V.4) may be inconsistent due to correlation between $\frac{x_t}{z_t}$, $\frac{x_{t+1}}{z_t}$, and $\phi^*(L) \frac{x_{t+1}}{z_t}$. Hence equations (V.5) and (V.6) would be our preferred equations and the implied elasticity of I/K with respect to q is between $1/2$ and $3/4$.

VI. Concluding Remarks

The purpose of this paper was to estimate an aggregate investment equation based on q, the ratio of the market value of capital to the cost of uninstalled capital goods. Rather than using stock market data to determine q, we used an implied series for q derived from the production function, wage rates and tax parameters. Relying on rational expectations, we then used this data to estimate the investment equation in a Koyck lead formulation. There is very strong evidence that q does indeed affect investment but the elasticity of investment with respect to q was not determined very precisely. It appears from the evidence in section V that the elasticity of the investment capital ratio with respect to q is somewhere between .5 and .75. A major problem in estimating this elasticity is that it was necessary to use the time series properties of x_t, the after-tax wage savings accruing to the marginal unit of capital, to extract an elasticity estimate from the coefficient estimates in the regressions. Although the estimated elasticity is not extremely sensitive to the order of the time series process used, there seems to be room for improvement in this technique. Unfortunately, the structural coefficient in which we are interested gets buried in a tangle of autoregressive parameters as a consequence of including a measure of the revisions in expectations as a regressor in the investment equation. However, this measure of revisions in expectations was included in an attempt to reduce the possible inconsistency arising from the use of imperfect instruments. Of course, if truly valid instruments could be found, i.e., instruments that are correlated with y_{t+1} and $\frac{x_t}{z_t}$, yet uncorrelated with the disturbance (including the revision in expectations), it would not be necessary to include the revision in expectations as a regressor.

Although the estimated investment equation appears to work well without expectational or delivery lags, it is not inconsistent with lags in the delivery of capital goods. We have observed that fluctuations in q generate fluctuations in the investment capital ratio. It is certainly possible, however, that the effect of q is distributed over several quarters. Since timing of the effects of policy is often a consideration in policy implementation, future work is necessary to determine the effect of lags in the installation of capital.

APPENDIX

Data Sources

The data used in this paper was taken largely from the MPS data bank. It is quarterly data over the period 1948-I to 1976-IV. The real output of the private domestic business nonfarm sector, X_t, was calculated as real gross private domestic business product (XB) minus real farm business output (XBF). Output in current dollars, $X\$_t$ was calculated as nonfarm business product and product of households (XBNF$) minus income originating in households (YH$). Total labor hours L_t was calculated as the sum of man-hours of employees, nonfarm business sector (LMHE) and proprietors' man-hours, nonfarm business sector (LMHS). In order to calculate a labor share of income, I used the employee compensation rate in nonfarm private domestic business (PL). As for the capital stock, I followed the example of the MPS model in calculating the stocks of durables and structures as the cumulation of past real investment net of depreciation. I used a depreciation rate of 6% per year for structures and 16% per year for durables, as in the MPS data bank. The gross investment series for structures and for durables were each adjusted so that the capital stock represents total nonfarm capital in constant dollars.

Construction of the Investment Series

The MPS model constructs the stock of structures according to the relation $KPS = .25EPS + KPS_{-1}(1 - UWPS/4.0)$, where KPS is the stock of producers' structures in constant dollars, EPS is the quarterly expenditure on producers' structures expressed at annual rates, and UWPS is the (constant) rate of depreciation of producers' structures. Rather than cumulating EPS, I have chosen to cumulate IS = ((EPS* - EPSF*)/EPS*)EPS, where EPS* is expenditure on private nonresidential structures (National Income and Product Accounts, Table 5.5, pp. 168-9, line 3), EPSF* is expenditure on private nonresidential farm structures (NIPA, pp. 168-9, line 18), and EPS is the MPS series on expenditure on producers' structures. Note that the asterisked data from the National Income and Product Accounts was available only annually. Hence, the average annual share on nonfarm investment was assumed to prevail in each of the four quarters. Similarly, the stock of nonfarm producers' durables was calculated as the cumulation of ID = ((EPD* - EPDF*)/EPD*)EPD, where EPD* is expenditure on nonresidential private producers' durables (NIPA, pp. 170-1, Table 5.7, line 2), EPDF* is expenditure on tractors and agricultural machinery except tractors (NIPA, pp. 170-1, Table 5.7, lines 6+7), and EPD is the MPS series on expenditure on producers' durables. Note that the data in NIPA ends in 1974. For 1975 and 1976 I assumed that the ratio of nonfarm investment to total investment remained at its 1974 level.

The cumulation formulas for the construction of the stocks of structures and durables require a benchmark. I chose 1948-I as the benchmark quarter. The MPS value for the stock of producers' structures for 1948-I was adjusted downward to remove farm structures, by multiplying the MPS value by the value of (EPS* - EPSF*)/EPS* in 1948. A similar adjustment was made for durables.

ESSAY III

FISCAL STIMULUS TO INVESTMENT:

TAX CUT OR INVESTMENT TAX CREDIT?

I. Introduction

Gross private capital formation has been very low for the past few years and economic policy makers are trying to decide upon appropriate policies to stimulate a recovery of investment expenditures. The two major tools being considered are a corporate tax cut and an increase in the investment tax credit. One basis for choice between these policies is the comparative costs of the policies in terms of lost tax revenue. In this paper, we develop a partial equilibrium framework to compare the tax revenues to the Treasury under a tax cut and an equivalent investment tax credit. This analysis is partial equilibrium in that we ignore the multiplier effects of increased investment as well as the interest rate effects of variations in the government deficit. In this paper, the schedule of demand for output is invariant to changes in the rate of investment, and the after-tax discount rate is invariant to the magnitude and financing of the government deficit. Within this framework, a permanent investment tax credit is shown to lead to a given increase in investment more cheaply than a permanent corporate tax cut. There is a presumption that this result holds also for temporary fiscal policies, although the result is not unambiguous in this case.

The analysis of this paper uses a variant of Tobin's q to explain investment behavior, as discussed in Essays I, II, and IV. The investment behavior of the firm is derived from explicit intertemporal optimization in a perfect foresight framework, and it is shown that investment is an increasing function of the shadow price of capital goods, adjusted for tax parameters. In Section II, we assume that the firm faces a horizontal demand curve for its output, as in Gould (1968). This is a very convenient formulation because the solution of the dynamic optimization problem is very easily tractable; indeed, the solution appears to be almost static. In this framework it is easily shown that tax revenue is higher under a permanent investment tax credit than under a permanent tax cut. In Section III, we assume that firms are sales constrained in the market for their output and thus face a fixed output constraint rather than a fixed price for output. The dynamic path to equilibrium is less static than in the fixed price case. However, the results concerning the relative costs of permanent fiscal policies are found to be qualitatively the same as in Section II. In Section IV, we compare the fixed price and fixed output cases and explain why the approach to steady state is more rapid in the latter case. In Section V, we study the effects of explicitly temporary fiscal policies in the fixed price case. There is no strong conclusion concerning the relative costs of the policies although there is a presumption that the qualitative results for permanent policies continue to hold for temporary policies of moderate magnitude. Section VI presents a discussion of temporary policies in the fixed output case and then generalizes the results to all types of demand curves and all durations of policy. However, the conclusions are unambiguous only for permanent policies. Concluding remarks are presented in Section VII.

II. The Fixed-Price Case

We assume that the representative firm acts to maximize the present value of its cash flow. The firm uses labor, L, and capital, K, to produce output which it can sell at the exogenously fixed price, P. Assuming that the production function is Cobb-Douglas, the total revenue of the firm is $PL^{\alpha}K^{1-\alpha}$, with the appropriate choice of units. Given the wage rate, w, and the corporate tax rate, τ, the after-tax operating profit of the firm is $(PL^{\alpha}K^{1-\alpha}-wL)(1-\tau)$. This constitutes one component of cash flow.

The second component of cash flow is net capital expenditures. Firms can buy uninstalled capital goods at a fixed price and then install the capital goods in place. The installation cost function is assumed to be a convex increasing function of the rate of investment, I. Thus, we may write the total cost of purchasing and installing capital goods at rate I as c(I), where $c'(I) > 0$ and $c''(I) > 0$. We also assume that $c(0) = 0$. Capital expenditures involve a gross cash outflow of c(I). However, there are two elements of the tax code which reduce the cash outflow. First, we consider the investment tax credit, which will be treated as an immediate rebate on the cost of adding to the capital stock. Let k be the rate of the investment tax credit. If the credit is allowed against installation costs as well as the purchase price of uninstalled capital goods, there is a cash inflow of kc(I).[1] Now we

---

[1]We assume that the original book value of installed capital goods which is used for tax purposes includes the installation costs. To the extent that installation costs are external to the firm rather than internal, this assumption seems justified.

consider the depreciation allowance. Let $D(x)$ be the depreciation allowance per unit of original book value for capital of age x. Then we define $z = \int_0^\infty D(x)e^{-rx}dx$ to be the present value of the depreciation deductions, where r is the after-tax rate of discount. Thus the present value of the cash inflow due to the depreciation allowance is $\tau zc(I)$.[1] Therefore, capital expenditures produce a net cash outflow of $(1 - k - \tau z)c(I)$. Now, for simplicity, we define $\beta = k + \tau z$, so that the cash outflow associated with investment expenditures is $(1 - \beta)c(I)$.[2]

Putting together all the elements of cash flow and assuming that w, P, and r are constant, we can write the firm's maximization problem as

$$\text{(II.1)} \qquad \max_{I,L} V = \int_0^\infty \{(PL_t^\alpha K_t^{1-\alpha} - wL_t)(1-\tau) - (1-\beta)c(I_t)\} e^{-rt}dt$$

subject to $\dot{K} = I - \delta K$. The Hamiltonian for this problem is

$$\text{(II.2)} \qquad H = e^{-rt}\{(PL_t^\alpha K_t^{1-\alpha} - wL_t)(1-\tau)-(1-\beta)c(I_t)\} + P_K e^{-rt}(I-\delta K)$$

Solving the first-order condition $\frac{\partial H}{\partial I} = 0$, we obtain

$$\text{(II.3)} \qquad c'(I) = P_K/(1-\beta) .$$

---

[1]Under the Long Amendment, it was necessary to subtract the investment tax credit from the original book value to arrive at the depreciation base, so that the present value of the depreciation allowance was $(1-k)\tau c(I)$. However, the Long Amendment was repealed in 1964, so that the expression in the text applies to the current tax regime.

[2]This formula holds for the tax regime under the Long Amendment if we define $\beta = k + \tau z - k\tau z$.

The right hand side of this equation may be interpreted as q, the ratio of the shadow price of installed capital to the (tax-adjusted) replacement cost of (uninstalled) capital, as explained in Essay I. Since $c'' > 0$, (II.3) shows that investment is an increase function of q.

Now solve the first-order condition $\frac{\partial H}{\partial L} = 0$ to obtain $(L/K) = (w/\alpha P)^{\frac{1}{\alpha-1}}$. Faced with a linearly homogeneous production function, the firm will always hire that amount of labor needed to make the labor-capital ratio equal to $(w/\alpha P)^{\frac{1}{\alpha-1}}$, which is exogenously determined. Solving the necessary condition $\frac{d}{dt}(P_K e^{-rt}) = \frac{-\partial H}{\partial K}$, we obtain

$$\text{(II.4)} \qquad \dot{P}_K = (r + \delta)P_K - (1 - \tau)\phi^* ,$$

where $\phi^* = (1 - \alpha)P(w/\alpha P)^{\frac{\alpha}{\alpha-1}}$ is the marginal revenue product of capital. Observe that the required return per unit of capital is $(r+\delta)P_K$ and that the realized return per unit of capital is the sum of the after-tax marginal revenue product, $(1-\tau)\phi^*$, and the capital gain, $\dot{P}_K$. Hence (II.4) expresses the equality of the realized and required returns on capital. Note that (II.4) is a differential equation governing the motion of P_K over time. The motion of the capital stock is given by

$$\text{(II.5)} \qquad \dot{K} = I - \delta K = c'^{-1}(P_K/(1-\beta)) - \delta K.$$

Before proceeding to the analysis of policy, we first study the steady state and the path to the steady state. We use an asterisk to denote steady state values. Setting $\dot{P}_K = 0$ in (II.4), we determine the steady state value of P_K to be

$$(\text{II.6}) \qquad P_K^* = (1 - \tau)\phi^*/(r + \delta).$$

That is, P_K^* is the present value of the stream of after-tax rentals accruing to a unit of capital installed today. Now setting $\dot{K} = 0$ in (II.5), the steady state value of the capital stock is

$$(\text{II.7}) \qquad K^* = \frac{1}{\delta} c'^{-1}((1 - \tau)\phi^*/[(r + \delta)(1 - \beta)]) .$$

Recall that ϕ^*, r, and δ are exogenously given so that the fiscal parameters τ and β determine the steady state capital stock. Note that for a given corporate tax rate τ, an increase in the rate of investment tax credit, k, increases β and hence increases K^*. Similarly, holding k constant and decreasing τ increases K^* so long as $z < 1 - k$, which is true empirically.[1]

To analyze the dynamics, we linearize the system around its steady state to obtain

$$(\text{II.8}) \qquad \begin{pmatrix} \dot{P}_K \\ \dot{K} \end{pmatrix} = \begin{pmatrix} r + \delta & 0 \\ \frac{1}{(1-\beta)c''(I^*)} & -\delta \end{pmatrix} \begin{pmatrix} P_K - P_K^* \\ K - K^* \end{pmatrix}$$

Note that if c(I) is quadratic in I, as in Gould (1968), then (II.8) is an exact representation of the system, without approximation. We shall

---

[1] Under the Long Amendment, the weaker condition that $z < 1$ is sufficient to insure $\frac{\partial K^*}{\partial \tau} < 0$.

use (II.8) for our analysis, viewing it either as an exact representation of a Gould system or as a linear approximation to a model with more general convex installation costs.[1] The phase diagram in Figure 1 shows the steady state and the vectors of motion. Note that the $\dot{P}_K = 0$ locus is horizontal since $\dot{P}_K$ is independent of the level of the capital stock. Recall from (II.4) that the capital gain $\dot{P}_K$ is equal to the required return $(r + \delta)P_K$ less the after-tax rental value of capital $(1 - \tau)\phi^*$. Since ϕ^* is independent of the level of the capital stock, $\dot{P}_K$ is independent of K also. As for the $\dot{K} = 0$ locus, it is upward sloping since a higher level of capital requires a higher rate of replacement investment which is called forth by a higher P_K. Drawing in the arrows of motion we find that the unique stable path to the saddle point steady state equilibrium is along the horizontal $\dot{P}_K = 0$ locus.

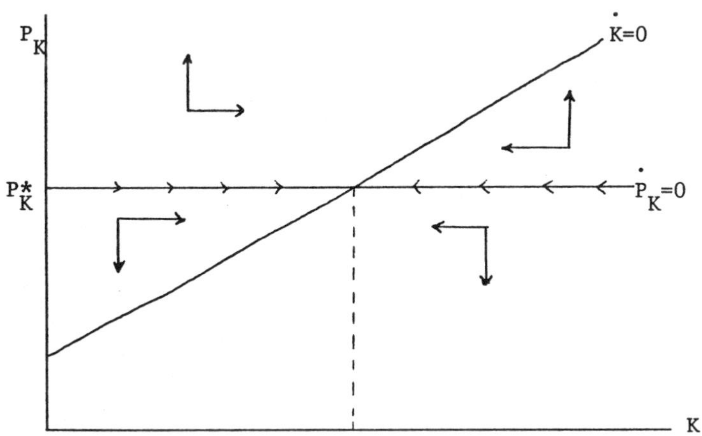

Figure 1

---

[1] We see below that P_K never deviates from P^*_K along the path to the steady state, so that I never deviates from I^*. Therefore $\dot{K}$ is linear in K, and (II.8) is an exact representation of the system.

The phase diagram tells us quite a lot about the path to steady state. Note that since P_K is constant along this path, the rate of investment is constant and equals its steady state value, i.e., $I = I^* = \delta K^*$. Furthermore, since $\dot{K} = I - \delta K$, we obtain

$$\text{(II.9)} \qquad \dot{K} = \delta(K^* - K).$$

That is, the growth rate of the capital stock is proportional to the gap between the steady state value and the current value of the capital stock. This result was obtained by Gould a decade ago, but his solution method was presented in a different manner. He used the transversality conditions to tie down the solution of a second-order differential equation.[1] On the other hand, the analysis of this paper is steeped in the tradition of the rational expectations literature which grew up after Gould's article was written. In the spirit of rational expectations, we realize that given the current level of the capital stock (and perfect foresight), there is a unique value for the price of capital which will allow the system to reach its steady state. The phase diagram with the stable path is used to determine this value of P_K. In this particular case, the choice of solution methods may be a matter of taste. In Section III, however, we examine a case in which the rational expectations approach to the solution appears preferable to direct solution of a second-order differential equation.

---

[1]Our system (II.8) appears to be a system of first-order differential equations in P_K and K. However, P_K is a function of $\dot{K}$ so that including $\dot{P}_K$ in the system makes it a second-order differential system in K.

One additional comment on the solution of this system is in order since it will help us to solve the system in Section III. Note that the roots of the matrix in (II.8) are $r + \delta$ and $-\delta$. These roots are used to characterize the solution of the system. If we impose the requirement that the system approaches its steady state, we must discard the positive root and obtain

$$\text{(II.10)} \qquad K_t = K^* + e^{-\delta t}(K^* - K_o) \ ,$$

where K_o is the initial capital stock. Differentiating with respect to time, we obtain

$$\text{(II.11)} \qquad \dot{K}_t = -\delta e^{-\delta t}(K^* - K_o) = \delta(K^* - K_t) \ ,$$

which is the Gould result once again.

Analysis of Policy

We now consider two alternative fiscal policies which increase the steady state level of the capital stock K^*. Suppose that the initial values of the corporate tax rate and the investment tax credit are τ_o and k_o, respectively. The first policy is a permanent investment tax credit which raises β to $\beta^{ITC} = k_1 + \tau_o z$. The second policy is a permanent corporate tax cut which reduces τ to τ_1 and reduces β to $\beta^{TX} = k_o + \tau_1 z$. We shall define equivalent policies as policies which lead to the same level of K^*. From (II.7), it is clear that equivalent policies are such that

$$(II.12)\qquad \frac{1-\tau_o}{1-\beta^{ITC}} = \frac{1-\tau_1}{1-\beta^{TX}}$$

Each of these policies leads to the same level of K^* and hence to the same rate of investment $I = \delta K^*$. Therefore, the time path of the capital stock is the same under the two policies. _A fortiori_, the time path of the pre-tax operating profit is the same under the two policies. It can be shown that at time t the pre-tax operating profit is $\phi^* K_t$.

Let R^{ITC} be the present value of tax revenue under the investment tax credit policy. Then

$$(II.13)\qquad R^{ITC} = \tau_o \int_0^\infty \phi^* K_t e^{-rt} dt - \beta^{ITC} \int_0^\infty c(I^*) e^{-rt} dt$$

Similarly, for the corporate tax cut, we obtain[1]

$$(II.14)\qquad R^{TX} = \tau_1 \int_0^\infty \phi^* K_t e^{-rt} dt - \beta^{TX} \int_0^\infty c(I^*) e^{-rt} dt$$

Now in order to determine which policy yields greater tax revenue, we examine the sign of

$$(II.15)\qquad R^{ITC} - R^{TX} = (\tau_o - \tau_1) \int_0^\infty \phi^* K_t e^{-rt} dt - (\beta^{ITC} - \beta^{TX}) \int_0^\infty c(I^*) e^{-rt} dt$$

---

[1]We use the after-tax discount rate r to evaluate the present value of tax revenues to the Treasury. It might be more appropriate to use the pre-tax rate $r/(1-\tau)$, which is nearly double the after-tax rate. However, considerations of risk premiums make us hesitate to use a higher discount rate to evaluate returns to the Treasury than to evaluate private sector returns. We have chosen to ignore these complications and use the same discount rate for the Treasury and for the private sector.

By rearranging (II.12), we obtain

$$\text{(II.16)} \qquad \beta^{ITC} - \beta^{TX} = \frac{\tau_o - \tau_1}{1 - \tau_o}(1 - \beta^{ITC})$$

Substituting (II.16) into (II.15) we obtain

$$\text{(II.17)} \qquad R^{ITC} - R^{TX} = \frac{\tau_o - \tau_1}{1-\tau_o}\{\int_0^\infty (1-\tau_o)\phi^* K_t e^{-rt}dt - (1-\beta^{ITC})\int_0^\infty c(I^*)e^{-rt}dt\}$$

Observe that the expression in brackets is the present value of the cash flow resulting from optimal behavior under an investment tax credit, i.e., V^{ITC}. Therefore,

$$\text{(II.18)} \qquad R^{ITC} - R^{TX} = \frac{\tau_o - \tau_1}{1 - \tau_o} V^{ITC}$$

We assume that the firm has a positive net present value so that $V^{ITC} > 0$. Since we are examining a tax cut, $\tau_o - \tau_1 > 0$. Finally, since $1 - \tau_1 > 0$, it is clear that $R^{ITC} > R^{TX}$. That is, an investment tax credit is less costly to the Treasury than is an equivalent tax cut.

We have shown formally that a corporate tax cut is more costly to the Treasury than an equivalent investment tax credit. Now we demonstrate this proposition in a more intuitively appealing manner. We assume that initially, the tax rate is equal to τ_o and that the investment tax credit rate is equal to k_o. The rate of investment is determined by (II.3) which we rewrite as

$$\text{(II.19)} \qquad (1-k_o - \tau_o z)c'(I) = P_K$$

This relation is illustrated in Figure 2. The net marginal investment cost function $(1-k_o-\tau_o z)c'(I)$ is an increasing function of I since the investment cost function c(I) is assumed to be convex. Note that P_K, the shadow price of installed capital, is equal to the present value of the after-tax rentals to capital, $\frac{(1-\tau_o)\phi^*}{r+\delta}$, and is invariant to the rate of investment. Thus it is represented as a horizontal line in Figure 2. The intersection of these schedules at point A yields the rate of investment, I_o.

Suppose that it is desired to raise investment to I_1. This target may be achieved by reducing the corporate tax rate to τ_1. With the lower tax rate, the shadow price of capital rises to $P_{K_1} = \frac{(1-\tau_1)\phi^*}{r+\delta}$. Also, since $1-k_o-\tau_1 z > 1-k_o-\tau_o z$, the net marginal investment cost function shifts upward in proportion to $\frac{(1-k_o-\tau_1 z)}{(1-k_o-\tau_o z)}$. Now, the intersection of the relevant curves is at point B, with the rate of investment equal to I_1.[1] An alternative policy to increase investment is to increase

[1]We know that B represents a higher rate of investment than the initial situation represented by A because $1-k > z$. In terms of Figure 2, the point B is farther to the right than point A because the new net marginal cost schedule $(1-k_o-\tau_1 z)c'(I)$, lies below the dotted line through point G. To show that this is true, we show that AE (the vertical distance between $(1-k_o-\tau_1 z)c'(I)$ and $(1-k_o-\tau_o z)c'(I)$ at I_o) is less than AG (the vertical distance between P_{K_1} and P_{K_o}.) Observe that $AE = (\tau_o-\tau_1)zc'(I_o)$ $=(\tau_o-\tau_1)z\,\frac{(1-\tau_o)\phi^*}{r+\delta}\,\frac{1}{1-k_o-\tau_o z}$. Also, observe that $AG = \frac{(\tau_o-\tau_1)\phi^*}{r+\delta}$. Therefore, AE is shorter than AG if and only if $\frac{z(1-\tau_o)}{1-k_o-\tau_o z} < 1$, i.e., if and only if $z < 1 - k_o$.

the investment tax credit from k_o to k_1. The higher level of k causes the upward sloping net marginal cost of investment schedule to shift downward in proportion to $\frac{(1-k_1-\tau_o z)}{(1-k_o-\tau_o z)}$. The new marginal cost schedule intersects the shadow price of capital at point C, with the rate of investment equal to I_1.

In Figure 2, we have represented equivalent fiscal stimuli to investment. Now we compare the tax revenues accruing to the Treasury under the two policies. Let RL be the present value of the tax revenue loss to the Treasury under the tax cut policy relative to the investment tax credit policy. One component of RL is the tax revenue loss on income accruing to existing capital in place due to the lower corporate tax rate. If K_t is the stock of existing capital, then $\frac{\phi^* K_t}{r+\delta}$ is the present value of income accruing to this capital. Therefore, $\frac{(\tau_o-\tau_1)\phi^*}{r+\delta} K_t$ is the tax revenue loss on existing capital. The second component of RL is the tax revenue loss on income accruing to capital installed over the future. In each interval of time, dt, the firm installs $I_1 dt$ units of capital which produce a present value of income of $\frac{\phi^*}{r+\delta} I_1 dt$ over the infinite future. The tax loss on income accruing to this increment of capital is $\frac{(\tau_o-\tau_1)\phi^*}{r+\delta} I_1 dt$. Since the rate of investment will be I_1 over the entire future, the present value of the tax loss on future investment is

$$\int_0^\infty \frac{(\tau_o-\tau_1)\phi^*}{r+\delta} I_1 e^{-rt} dt = \frac{(\tau_o-\tau_1)\phi^*}{r+\delta} \frac{I_1}{r} .$$

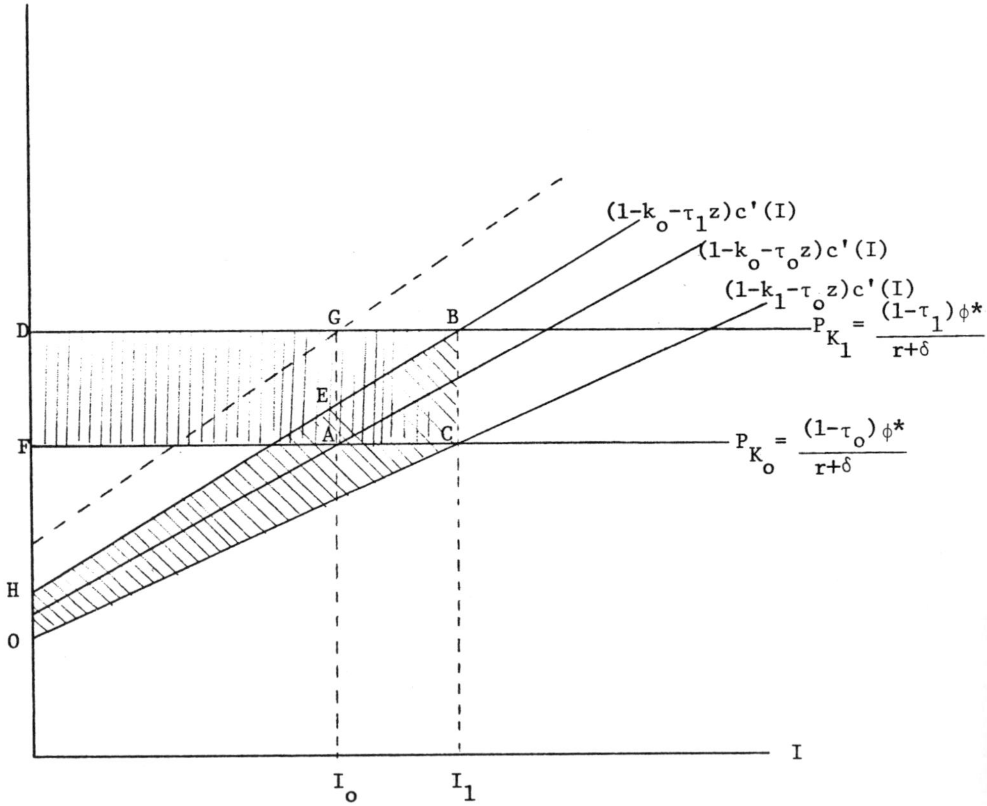
$(1-k_o-\tau_1 z)c'(I)$
$(1-k_o-\tau_o z)c'(I)$
$(1-k_1-\tau_o z)c'(I)$
$P_{K_1} = \frac{(1-\tau_1)\phi^*}{r+\delta}$
$P_{K_o} = \frac{(1-\tau_o)\phi^*}{r+\delta}$
D
F
H
O
G
B
E
A
C
I
I_o
I_1

Figure 2

In addition to the two positive components of RL, $\frac{(\tau_o-\tau_1)\phi^*}{r+\delta} K_t$ and $\frac{(\tau_o-\tau_1)\phi^*}{r+\delta} \frac{I_1}{r}$, there is a negative component of RL due to the investment tax credit and the depreciation allowance. In any future interval of time dt, the investment tax credit and the depreciation allowance save firms $(k_o+\tau_1 z)c(I_1)dt$ under the tax cut policy and $(k_1+\tau_o z)c(I_1)dt$ under the investment tax credit policy. Since $k_o < k_1$ and $\tau_1 < \tau_o$, the Treasury returns less tax revenue to firms under the tax cut policy than under the investment tax credit policy. The present value of the Treasury's tax revenue gain under the tax cut vis-a-vis the investment tax credit is $\frac{1}{r}[(k_1 + \tau_o z) - (k_o + \tau_1 z)]c(I_1)$. Subtracting this revenue gain from the two positive components of the revenue loss above we obtain[1]

$$\text{(II.20)} \quad RL = \frac{(\tau_o-\tau_1)\phi^*}{r+\delta} K_t + \frac{1}{r}\{\frac{(\tau_o-\tau_1)\phi^*}{r+\delta} I_1 - ((k_1+\tau_o z)-(k_o+\tau_1 z))c(I_1)\}$$

The first term on the right hand side is the tax revenue loss on income accruing to capital already in place. This term is greater than zero.

[1]We have ignored the negative contribution to RL due to the remaining depreciation allowances on existing capital. The lower tax rate under the tax cut policy would mean that firms receive a lower tax saving from the depreciation allowance, vis-a-vis the investment tax credit and that the Treasury's tax revenue would be greater. However, as long as the remaining allowable depreciation deductions on existing capital are not so large as to create negative taxable income from existing capital, the tax cut causes a reduction in taxes on existing capital and our results still hold. In any case, our results hold after a transition period equal to the tax life of capital.

To determine the algebraic sign of the second term on the right hand side we examine Figure 2. Note that $\frac{(\tau_o-\tau_1)\phi^*}{r+\delta} = P_{K_1} - P_{K_o}$ so that $\frac{(\tau_o-\tau_1)\phi^*}{r+\delta} I_1 = (P_{K_1} - P_{K_o})I_1$ is equal to the area of the shaded rectangle FCBD in Figure 2. We observe that $((k_1+\tau_o z) - (k_o+\tau_1 z))c(I_1)$ equals the area of the shaded region OHBC in Figure 2, since this area is equal to

$$\int_0^{I_1} [(1-k_1-\tau_o z)c'(I) - (1-k_o-\tau_1 z)c'(I)]dI = ((k_1+\tau_o z) - (k_o+\tau_1 z))c(I_1).$$

Hence, the second term on the right hand side of (II.20) will be positive if and only if the area of rectangle FCBD exceeds the area of region OHBC. This condition is clearly satisfied since the two regions have the same horizontal length and the rectangle has a greater vertical width than OHBC everywhere except along the common edge BC where they have equal width.[1] Therefore, the second term on the right hand side of (II.20) is positive also. Hence, RL is positive so that the tax revenue accruing to the Treasury under an investment tax credit is greater than under an equivalent corporate tax cut.

To summarize, the tax revenue loss to the Treasury is smaller under an investment tax credit than under an equivalent corporate tax cut for two reasons. First, a corporate tax cut causes a loss of tax revenue on

---

[1]If $c(I)$ is quadratic without a linear or constant term, then $c'(I)$ is linear and passes through the origin. Therefore, region OHBC is a triangle and its area is equal to one half of the area of rectangle FCBD.

income accruing to existing capital in place. However, the tax revenues under the investment tax credit are not affected at all by existing capital. Secondly, the net tax revenue on future investment is higher under the investment tax cut as shown in Figure 2 because the marginal tax credit incentive, $(k_1-k_o)c'(I)$ is greater than the average tax credit $(k_1-k_o)c(I)/I$. However, under the tax cut policy, the marginal corporate tax break $\frac{(\tau_o-\tau_1)\phi^*}{r+\delta} - (\tau_o-\tau_1)zc'(I)$ is less than the average corporate tax break $\frac{(\tau_o-\tau_1)\phi^*}{r+\delta} - \frac{(\tau_o-\tau_1)zc(I)}{I}$.

Since the marginal tax credit equals the marginal corporate tax break under equivalent policies, the average tax credit is less than the average corporate tax break. Hence, from the point of view of the Treasury, the investment tax credit is cheaper than an equivalent corporate tax cut.[1]

III. The Fixed Output Case

In Section II, we studied the case in which the representative firm faces a horizontal demand curve for its output. Now we consider the polar opposite case in which firms face a binding sales constraint. We assume that the sales constraint has the constant value $\bar{Q}$ over the entire

---

[1]If the book value of capital upon which the investment tax credit and the depreciation allowance are based does not include installation costs, but rather is equal to the constant purchase price of uninstalled capital goods, the tax revenue loss on future investment is equal under the two equivalent policies. However, the investment tax credit is still cheaper from the Treasury's viewpoint because of the tax loss under a tax cut on income accruing to existing capital.

future, so that the firm produces $\bar{Q}$ at every point of time.[1] Since the capital stock is fixed at any instant of time, the labor input is $\bar{Q}^{1/\alpha} K_t^{1-1/\alpha}$ so that the labor and capital can be used to produce output $\bar{Q}$. The maximization problem is thus

$$\text{(III.1)} \qquad \max_{I} V = \int_0^\infty \{(\bar{Q}-w\bar{Q}^{1/\alpha}K^{1-1/\alpha})(1-\tau) - (1-\beta)c(I)\}e^{-rt}dt$$

subject to $\dot{K} = I - \delta K$. Setting up the Hamiltonian and solving $\frac{\partial H}{\partial I} = 0$, we obtain

$$\text{(III.2)} \qquad c'(I) = \frac{P_K}{1-\beta} \text{ as in Section II .}$$

Solving the necessary condition $\frac{d}{dt}(P_K e^{-rt}) = \frac{-\partial H}{\partial K}$, we obtain

$$\text{(III.3)} \qquad \dot{P}_K = (r+\delta)P_K - (1-\tau)\frac{1-\alpha}{\alpha} w(\frac{\bar{Q}}{K})^{1/\alpha}$$

As in Section II, this equation may be interpretated as the equality of the required return on capital, $(r+\delta)P_K$, with the realized return on capital, $(1-\tau)\frac{1-\alpha}{\alpha} w (\frac{\bar{Q}}{A})^{1/\alpha} + \dot{P}_K$.

This equation governs the motion of P_K. The capital stock changes according to

---

[1]This constraint will be binding if $K > (\frac{\alpha}{w/P})^{\alpha/1-\alpha}$ $\bar{Q}$, that is, if $\bar{Q}/K$ is sufficiently small. We assume that this condition holds at all points of time.

$$(\text{III.4}) \qquad \dot{K} = c'^{-1}(P_K/(1-\beta)) - \delta K \ .$$

We may now establish certain steady state relationships and then linearize our system around the steady state to analyze its dynamics. Setting $\dot{K} = 0$ in (III.4), we obtain

$$(\text{III.5}) \qquad I^* = \delta K^* \ ,$$

and setting $\dot{P}_K = 0$ in (III.3), we obtain

$$(\text{III.6}) \qquad P_K^* = \frac{1-\tau}{r+\delta}\,\frac{1-\alpha}{\alpha}\, w \left(\frac{\bar{Q}}{K^*}\right)^{1/\alpha}$$

Linearizing the two-equation system around the steady state we obtain

$$(\text{III.7}) \qquad \begin{pmatrix} \dot{P}_K \\ \dot{K} \end{pmatrix} = \begin{pmatrix} r+\delta & \dfrac{(r+\delta)P_K^*}{\alpha K^*} \\ \dfrac{1}{(1-\beta)c''(I^*)} & -\delta \end{pmatrix} \begin{pmatrix} P_K - P_K^* \\ K - K^* \end{pmatrix}$$

Now consider an increase in the investment tax credit rate and an equivalent decrease in the corporate tax rate. Recall that we have defined equivalent policies as those leading to the same steady state capital stock K^*. Hence the policies lead to the same steady state investment $I^* = \delta K^*$. Since $c'(I^*) = P_K^*/(1-\beta)$, these policies lead to the same values for $P_K^*/(1-\beta)$. Hence, we obtain

$$(\text{III.8}) \qquad \frac{1-\tau_o}{1-\beta^{ITC}} = \frac{1-\tau_1}{1-\beta^{TX}}$$

using (III.6) to substitute for P_K^*. Note that this relationship between equivalent policies is the same as in Section II.

Since the two alternative policies lead to the same steady state capital stock, any difference in their effects on the capital stock must be in the approach to steady state. To examine the approach to long-run equilibrium, we must examine the roots of the system. The characteristic equation of the matrix in (III.7) is

$$\text{(III.9)} \qquad \lambda^2 - r\lambda - (r+\delta)[\delta + \frac{P_K^*}{\alpha K^*} \frac{1}{(1-\beta)c''(I^*)}]$$

Using the quadratic formula to solve for the roots of this equation, we obtain

$$\text{(III.10)} \qquad \lambda = \frac{r \pm \sqrt{(r+2\delta)^2 + 4(r+\delta)\dfrac{P_K^*}{(1-\beta)\alpha K^* c''(I^*)}}}{2}$$

Examination of (III.10) reveals several interesting results. Since K^*, $c''(I^*)$ and $P_K^*/(1-\beta)$ are identical for the two policies, the roots of the system are the same for the two policies. Furthermore, one root is positive and one root is negative so that if the system is to reach its steady state, the movement of the capital stock is governed entirely by the one negative root. Under either policy,

$$\text{(III.11)} \qquad K_t = K^* + e^{\lambda^* t}(K^* - K_o) ,$$

where λ^* is the negative root. Differentiating (III.11) with respect to time and rearranging, we find that

$$(III.12) \qquad \dot{K}_t = -\lambda^*(K^* - K_t) \, .$$

Recalling that $-\lambda^*$ is positive, we once again have the result that the capital stock moves toward K^* at a rate proportional to the gap $K^* - K_t$. This result is more general than the result presented by Gould. In general, if the linearized system of a perfect foresight system has only one negative root so that the steady state is a saddle point equilibrium, then all state variables approach their steady state values at a rate proportional to the distance from equilibrium.[1] The Gould model, as presented in Section II, is seen to be a special case with the negative root equal to $-\delta$. In this section of the paper, with firms facing a sales constraint, the negative root is seen from (III.10) to be algebraically less than $-\delta$. Therefore, the approach to equilibrium is faster than in the fixed-price case.[2]

Now we compare the tax revenues under the two equivalent policies. Having established that the policies lead to the same time path of the capital stock, we may follow the calculations of Section II to obtain

$$(III.13) \qquad R^{ITC} - R^{TX} = \frac{\tau_o - \tau_1}{1-\tau_o} V^{ITC} > 0$$

Hence, once again, an investment tax credit is seen to be less costly to the Treasury than an equivalent corporate tax cut.

---

[1]See Lucas (1967) and Treadway (1974).

[2]See Section IV for an explanation of the relative speeds of approach to equilibrium in the two cases.

IV. Comparison of the Speeds of Approach to Steady State in the Fixed Price Case and the Fixed Output Case

In Section III it was shown by examination of the roots of the system that the approach to steady state is more rapid in the output constrained case than in the fixed price case. In this section, we present a more intuitive explanation of this result. Ignoring taxes and the investment tax credit, investment is an increasing function of P_K, the shadow price of installed capital goods. We show that along the path to the steady state, P_K is higher in the output constrained case than in the fixed price case, given that the steady state is the same in each case. Therefore, the approach to steady state is faster in the output-constrained case.

Let ρ_s be the rental price of capital at time s. Then the shadow price of installed capital (an asset price) at time t is

$$(IV.1) \qquad P_{K_t} = \int_t^{\infty} \rho_s e^{-\delta(r+\delta)(s-t)} ds \quad .$$

That is, if a unit of capital is installed at time t, then at time s, there is $e^{-\delta(s-t)}$ units of capital which earn a rental of $\rho_s e^{-\delta(s-t)}$. The present value of these rental returns is equal to P_K.

Now we consider the fixed price case which we refer to as case 1. (The superscript 1 will denote case 1.) In this case, the rental to capital is equal to the output price multiplied by the marginal physical product of capital,

$$(IV.2) \qquad \rho_s^{(1)} = \frac{(1-\alpha)PQ_s}{K_s}$$

where Q_s is the value of output at time s. Assuming competitive factor markets so that $\alpha PQ_s = wL_s$, we obtain

$$(IV.3) \qquad \rho_s^{(1)} = \frac{1-\alpha}{\alpha} w \frac{L_s}{K_s}$$

Recall from Section II that with fixed P and w, the labor capital ratio is fixed over time so that $\rho_s^{(1)}$ is constant for all s.

Now consider case 2 in which $\bar{Q}$ is the exogenously fixed level of the (constant) output constraint. In this case, the rental price of capital is equal to the wage rate multiplied by the marginal rate of substitution of labor for capital,

$$(IV.4) \qquad \rho_s^{(2)} = \frac{1-\alpha}{\alpha} w \left(\frac{\bar{Q}}{K_s}\right)^{1/\alpha}$$

Assuming that the initial capital stock is below its steady state level, K_s grows over time and hence $\rho_s^{(2)}$ falls over time. Note that by substituting the production relationship into (IV.4), we obtain the rental as a function of the labor capital ratio

$$(IV.5) \qquad \rho_s^{(2)} = \frac{1-\alpha}{\alpha} w \frac{L_s}{K_s}$$

A comparison of (IV.3) and (IV.5) shows that the rental is the same function of the labor capital ratio in the two cases. However, in the fixed price case, the labor capital ratio is $(\frac{w}{\alpha P})^{1/\alpha-1}$ which is constant over time. In the fixed output case, as K_s grows, L_s shrinks, so the labor capital ratio shrinks over time.

Comparison of Rentals for the Same Wage Rate

In this subsection we compare the rental rates when the two types of firms face the same wage rate, and the same price of output. Recall that the marginal revenue product of labor, MP_{L_s}, given the level of the capital stock, is a decreasing function of labor usage, as shown in Figure 3. The price-taking unconstrained firm uses $L^{(1)}$ of labor so that the marginal revenue product of labor equals the fixed nominal wage. However, for the output constrained case, the marginal revenue product of labor curve is given by ABC. The marginal revenue product curve becomes vertical at $L^{(2)}$ because, when $L = L^{(2)}$, the firm hits its output constraint and cannot use more labor to produce any additional revenue. Note that $L^{(2)} < L^{(1)}$ and that the marginal revenue product of labor at $L^{(2)}$ exceeds the fixed wage rate. This inequality of the marginal revenue product of labor and the wage rate is the manifestation of the output

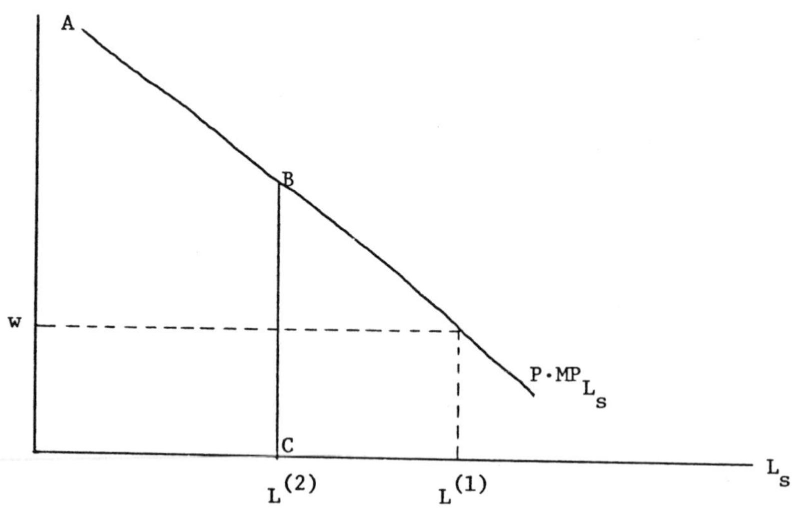

Figure 3

constraint. Given the capital stock and the real wage rate, the firm would like to use more labor and sell more output, but it is prevented from doing so. Since this figure is drawn for a given capital stock,

it is clear that $\rho_s^{(1)} = \frac{1-\alpha}{\alpha} w \frac{L_s^{(1)}}{K_s} > \frac{1-\alpha}{\alpha} w \frac{L_s^{(2)}}{K_s} = \rho_s^{(2)}$.

The only way for $\rho_s^{(1)}$ to equal $\rho_s^{(2)}$ when the capital stock is the same in both cases is for the wage rate to be higher in case 1 than in case 2. The higher wage rate $w^{(1)}$ will reduce output in case 1, and since $w^{(1)}L^{(1)} = \alpha PQ$, $w^{(1)}L^{(1)}$ will be reduced.[2] An appropriate increase in w^1 will reduce w^1L^1 enough to bring it into equality with $w^{(2)}L^{(2)}$.

Comparison of Cases With Identical Steady States

We now compare cases 1 and 2 for situations in which the steady state is the same. Since the steady state capital stock K^* is the same in both cases, the steady state replacement investment, δK^*, is the same in both cases. The same replacement investment requires $P_K^{*(1)} = P_K^{*(2)}$.

Clearly, since $P_K^* = \frac{\rho^*}{(r+\delta)}$, $P_K^{*(1)} = P_K^{*(2)}$ if and only if $\rho^{*(1)} = \rho^{*(2)}$.

Thus the steady state rentals to capital are the same in the two cases. However, for the fixed-price case $\rho_s = \rho^*$ for all s, whereas in the output constrained case ρ_s falls smoothly over time to ρ^*. The time paths of the rental rates are in Figure 4. The shadow price of installed capital goods is equal to the discounted area under the rental curve.[1]

---

[1]The discount factor is r+δ, reflecting both time preference and physical depreciation.

[2]A lower price P, which raises the real wage rate w/P, will have the same effect.

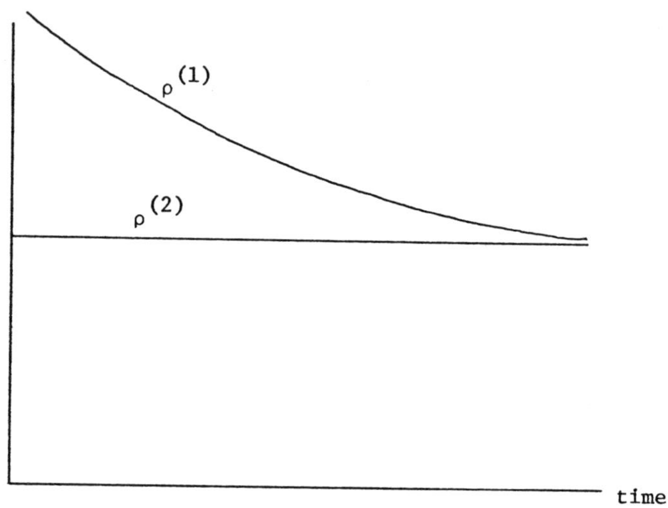

Figure 4

Clearly, $P_K^{(2)} > P_K^{(1)} = P_K^*$ whenever the capital stock is below its steady state value. We recall that in the fixed price case, investment is always equal to δK^* so that $c'(\delta K^*) = P_K^{*(1)}$. However, in the output constrained case, investment exceeds δK^* along the path to steady state. Suppose that investment were equal to δK^* in the fixed output case. Then $c'(I) = c'(\delta K^*) = P_K^{*(2)} < P_K^{(2)}$ which violates the condition $c'(I) = P_K^{(2)}$. But if investment increases, then c'(I) increases; so I rises until $c'(I) = P_K$. If a higher rate of investment is maintained for more than an infinitesimal interval of time, the time path of the capital stock will be higher, the time path of rentals will be lower and hence the shadow price of installed capital will be lower. However, the shadow price of installed capital is always above P_K^* as long as $K_t < K^*$. Thus, since $c'(I) = P_K$, investment will exceed the steady state rate of investment when $K_t < K^*$, and the approach to the steady state is more rapid in the output constrained case than in the fixed price case.

V. Temporary Fiscal Policies in the Fixed Price Case

In Section II, we examined the effect of permanent changes in the tax code on the investment behavior of price-taking firms and compared the tax revenue under the different policies. In this section we discuss the effect of temporary fiscal policies. The analysis of this section is complicated by the fact that the present value of the cash flow attributable to the depreciation allowance can no longer be easily summarized by the time-invariant expression $\tau z = \tau \int_t^\infty D(s-t)e^{-r(s-t)}ds.$[1]

---

[1]Recall from Section II that D(x) is the per unit depreciation allowance for capital of age x.

This formula is merely a special case of $\int_t^{\infty} \tau_s D(s-t)e^{-r(s-t)}ds$ in which the corporate tax rate τ_s is constant. When considering temporary tax rate changes, we can no longer assume that τ_s is constant over the entire future. However, in this section we will restrict our attention to tax policies of the form: $\tau_s = \tau_1$ for $t \leq s < t^*$ and $\tau_s = \tau_o$ for $s \geq t^*$. Then the present value of the depreciation allowance may be written as

$$\text{(V.1)} \qquad \tau_1 \hat{D}(t^* - t) + \tau_o \hat{\hat{D}}(t^* - t), \text{ where}$$

$$\hat{D} = \int_t^{t^*} D(s-t)e^{-r(s-t)}ds, \quad \hat{\hat{D}} = \int_{t^*}^{\infty} D(s-t)e^{-r(s-t)}ds, \quad \text{and } \hat{D} + \hat{\hat{D}} = z \ .$$

As is clear from (V.1), the present value of the depreciation allowance is a function of (t-t*), the amount of time remaining until the temporary tax change is removed. Note that $\frac{d}{d(t^*-t)} \hat{D}(t^*-t) = D(t^*-t)e^{-r(t^*-t)}$ and $\frac{d}{d(t^*-t)} \hat{\hat{D}}(t^*-t) = -D(t^*-t)e^{-r(t^*-t)}$ so that

$$\text{(V.2)} \qquad \frac{d}{d(t^*-t)} (\tau_1 \hat{D} + \tau_o \hat{\hat{D}}) = (\tau_1 - \tau_o)D(t^* - t)e^{-r(t^*-t)}$$

We will consider the case of a temporary decrease in the corporate tax rate so that $\tau_1 < \tau_o$. Note that as time passes, the remaining life of the tax cut, t*-t, decreases, so that the rate of change of the present value of the depreciation allowance is given by

$$\text{(V.3)} \qquad \frac{-\,d}{d(t^*-t)}\,(\tau_1\hat{D} + \tau_o\hat{\hat{D}}) = (\tau_o - \tau_1)D(t^* - t)e^{-r(t^*-t)} > 0.$$

To summarize briefly, a temporary decrease in the corporate tax rate causes an immediate discontinuous downward drop in the present value of the depreciation allowance. Then as time passes and we approach the date when the original tax regime is restored, the present value of the depreciation allowance rises smoothly toward its original value.

The Effect on Investment of a Decrease in the Corporate Tax Rate

We established earlier that $c'(I) = P_K/(1-\beta)$, so that investment is an increasing function of the contemporaneous value of $P_K/(1-\beta)$. Thus the effects of policy on investment are qualitatively the same as the effects on $P_K/(1-\beta)$. For convenience, we focus our attention on the effects of fiscal policy on $P_K/(1-\beta)$.

Recall from Section IV that P_K is the present value of the after-tax rentals accruing to the undepreciated portion of a unit of capital installed today, at time t. Since the pre-tax rental in the fixed-price case is ϕ^*, we obtain

$$\text{(V.4)} \qquad P_K = \int_t^{t^*} (1-\tau_1)\phi^* e^{-(r+\delta)(s-t)}ds + \int_{t^*}^{\infty} (1-\tau_o)\phi^* e^{-(r+\delta)(s-t)}ds$$

$$= \frac{(1-\tau_1)\phi^*}{r+\delta} - \frac{(\tau_o-\tau_1)\phi^*}{r+\delta}\, e^{-(r+\delta)(t^*-t)}$$

Note that P_K is greater than $\frac{(1-\tau_o)\phi^*}{r+\delta}$ which was its value in the original regime. Taking the derivative of (V.4) with respect to time we obtain

$$(V.5) \qquad \dot{P}_K = -(\tau_o - \tau_1)\phi^* e^{-(r+\delta)(t^*-t)}$$

The shadow price of installed capital goods falls over time as we approach the date when the after-tax rentals fall from $(1-\tau_1)\phi^*$ to $(1-\tau_o)\phi^*$.

Now that we have examined the effect of a tax cut on the numerator of $P_K/(1-\beta)$, we examine the denominator. Recall that β is the sum of the investment tax credit k_o and the present value of the depreciation allowance, $\tau_1\hat{D} + \tau_o\hat{\hat{D}}$. Hence,

$$(V.6) \qquad 1 - \beta_s = 1-k_o - \tau_1\hat{D}(t^*-s) - \tau_o\hat{\hat{D}}(t^*-s) \qquad t \leq s < t^*$$

Note that reducing τ_1 from its original value of τ_o increases $1 - \beta_s$. As explained above, the present value of the depreciation allowance increases over time so that $1 - \beta_s$ falls smoothly over time. Thus in response to a temporary reduction in the corporate tax rate, both the numerator and denominator of $P_K/(1-\beta)$ jump upward and then fall smoothly over time. Therefore, further analysis is required to determine the effects on $P_K/(1-\beta)$.

We first examine the instantaneous effect of a decrease in the tax rate on $P_K/(1-\beta)$. We evaluate $\frac{\partial}{\partial\tau_1}(\frac{P_K}{1-\beta})$ assuming that the initial value of τ_1 is equal to τ_o. Note that $\frac{\partial}{\partial\tau_1}(\frac{P_K}{1-\beta})$ is equal to

$\{(1-\beta)\frac{\partial P_K}{\partial\tau_1} + P_K\frac{\partial\beta}{\partial\tau_1}\}/(1-\beta)^2$. Taking the indicated derivatives, we obtain

$$\text{(V.7)} \qquad \frac{\partial}{\partial\tau_1}\left(\frac{P_K}{1-\beta}\right) = \frac{\phi^*}{r+\delta}\{(1-k_o-\tau_1\hat{D}-\tau_o\hat{\hat{D}})(-1+e^{-(r+\delta)(t^*-t)} + (1-\tau_1+(\tau_1-\tau_o)e^{-(r+\delta)(t^*-t)})\hat{D}\}/(1-\beta)^2$$

Recalling that $\hat{D} + \hat{\hat{D}} = z$, we can simplify (V.7) to obtain

$$\text{(V.8)} \qquad \frac{\partial}{\partial\tau_1}\left(\frac{P_K}{1-\beta}\right) = \frac{-\phi^*}{r+\delta}\{(1-k_o-z)(1-e^{-(r+\delta)(t^*-t)}) + (1-\tau_o)A\}/(1-\beta)^2$$

where $A = \hat{\hat{D}}(1-e^{-(r+\delta)(t^*-t)}) - \hat{D}(e^{-(r+\delta)(t^*-t)})$

Now, $\frac{\partial}{\partial\tau_1}\left(\frac{P_K}{1-\beta}\right)$ will be negative if and only if the term in brackets in (V.8) is positive. The first term, $(1-k_o-z)(1-e^{-(r+\delta)(t^*-t)})$ is positive if we retain the assumption from Section II that $z < 1 - k_o$. Thus, a sufficient condition for a temporary increase in the corporate tax rate to reduce $P_K/(1-\beta)$ is that A be greater than or equal to zero. The sign of A depends on the depreciation allowance schedule. If the depreciation allowance for tax purposes is proportional to physical depreciation, i.e., $D(x) = \lambda e^{-\delta x}$, then we can easily calculate (V.9) $\hat{D} = \frac{\lambda}{r+\delta}(1-e^{-(r+\delta)(t^*-t)}$,

$$\text{(V.9)} \qquad \hat{D} = \frac{\lambda}{r+\delta}(1-e^{-(r+\delta)(t^*-t)}) \quad ; \quad \hat{\hat{D}} = \frac{\lambda}{r+\delta}e^{-(r+\delta)(\tau^*-\tau)}$$

Substituting (V.9) into the definition of A, we find that A = 0. If the depreciation allowance schedule is less rapidly declining than physical depreciation, the ratio $\hat{D}/\hat{\hat{D}}$ is less than $(1-e^{-(r+\delta)(t^*-t)})/e^{-(r+\delta)(t^*-t)}$, and A is positive. Thus if accounting

---

[1]We require that λ lie between 0 and $(1-k_o)(r+\delta)$ so that

$$0 < z = \hat{D} + \hat{\hat{D}} = \frac{\lambda}{r+\delta} < 1 - k_o.$$

depreciation for tax purposes is proportional to, or more slowly declining than, physical depreciation, $\frac{\partial}{\partial\tau_1}(\frac{P_K}{1-\beta})$ is negative. Therefore, a temporary corporate tax cut raises investment. However, under very accelerated depreciation allowance schedules in which D(x) falls rapidly with x, it is possible for a temporary tax cut to reduce investment. These results should not be construed to mean that accelerated depreciation lowers investment. Rather, they imply that under an accelerated depreciation allowance regime, a tax rise rather than a tax cut may be required to raise investment.

The question naturally arises how the response of $P_K/(1-\beta)$ to a temporary tax cut compares with the response to a permanent tax cut. Restricting our attention to the case in which the depreciation allowance is proportional to physical depreciation, we note that (V.8) may be rewritten as

$$\text{(V.10)} \qquad \frac{\partial}{\partial\tau_1}\left(\frac{P_K}{1-\beta}\right) = \frac{-\phi^*}{(r+\delta)(1-\beta)^2}(1-k_o-z)\frac{\hat{D}}{z}$$

since in this case, $A = 0$ and $\hat{D}/z = (1 - e^{-(r+\delta)(t^*-t)})$. Now, for a permanent tax cut, we can easily obtain

$$\text{(V.11)} \qquad \frac{\partial}{\partial\tau_1}\left(\frac{P_K}{1-\beta}\right) = \frac{-\phi^*}{(r+\delta)(1-\beta)^2}(1-k_o-z).$$

Note that the magnitude of the jump is greater for a permanent tax cut than for a temporary tax cut. From (V.10), it is easily seen that as the duration of the tax cut is increases, $\hat{D}/z$ increases, and hence the magnitude of the jump increases. In the limiting case of a permanent tax cut, $\hat{D}/z$ equals one and (V.10) reduces to (V.11).

Now that we have determined how $P_K/(1-\beta)$ jumps when a temporary tax cut is enacted, we examine how this ratio behaves for the duration of the tax cut. Note that the sign of $\frac{\partial}{\partial t}(\frac{P_K}{1-\beta})_s$ is the same as the sign of $(1-\beta_s)(\dot{P}_K)_s + (P_K)_s\dot{\beta}_s$. Using equations (V.3), (V.4) and (V.5), it is easily determined that

$$(V.12) \qquad (1-\beta_s)\dot{P}_K + P_K\dot{\beta}_s = -(1-\beta_s)(\tau_o-\tau_1)\phi^* e^{-(r+\delta)(t^*-s)}$$

$$+ [1-\tau_1 - (\tau_o-\tau_1)e^{-(r+\delta)(t^*-s)}]\frac{\phi^*}{r+\delta}(\tau_o-\tau_1)D(t^*-t)^{-r(t^*-s)},$$

$$t \leq s < t^* .$$

We assume that accounting depreciation for tax purposes is proportional to physical depreciation so that $\hat{D}(t^*-s)$ and $\hat{\hat{D}}(t^*-s)$ are given by (V.9) with s replacing t. Substituting $\lambda e^{-\delta(t^*-s)}$ for $D(t^*-s)$, and using (V.6) to substitute for $1-\beta_s$, we obtain

$$(V.13) \qquad (1-\beta_s)\dot{P}_K + P_K\dot{\beta} = -(\tau_o-\tau_1)\phi^* e^{-(r+\delta)(t^*-s)}(1-k_o-z) < 0 ,$$

$$t \leq s < t^*$$

Therefore, $(\frac{P_K}{1-\beta})_s$ falls over time for $t \leq s < t^*$.

To summarize the manipulations above, we have determined how $\frac{P_K}{(1-\beta)}$ responds to a temporary tax cut. If the depreciation allowance is equal to physical depreciation, then a temporary tax cut causes an immediate upward jump in $\frac{P_K}{(1-\beta)}$. The magnitude of the jump in $\frac{P_K}{(1-\beta)}$ is smaller for a temporary tax cut than for a permanent tax cut of the same size. After jumping upward, this ratio falls smoothly over time until time t* when the original tax rate is restored. At this time, $\frac{P_K}{(1-\beta)}$ reaches its steady state value of $\frac{(1-\tau_o)\phi^*}{(r+\delta)(1-k_o-\tau_o z)}$.

Comparison of a Tax Cut and Investment Tax Credit

Thus far in this section we have examined only a temporary tax cut. We will now show that for any tax cut of the form described above, there is an equivalent time pattern of the investment tax credit. The investment tax credit is equivalent to the tax cut in the sense that it leads to the same value of $\frac{P_K}{(1-\beta)}$ at every point of time. Note that an investment tax credit does not affect the stream of after-tax rentals to capital so that P_K remains equal to $\frac{(1-\tau_o)\phi^*}{r+\delta}$. Thus in order to maintain equality between $(P_K/(1-\beta))^{TX}$ and $(P_K/1-\beta))^{ITC}$, the denominator of this ratio is controlled by changing the rate of the investment tax credit. Imposing the restriction that $\frac{P_K}{(1-\beta)}$ is the same under the two policies, we obtain

$$\text{(V.14)} \qquad \frac{1-\tau_1 - (\tau_o-\tau_1)e^{-(r+\delta)(t^*-s)}}{1 - \beta_s^{TX}} = \frac{1 - \tau_o}{1 - \beta_s^{ITC}} \qquad \text{for } t \leq s < t^*$$

This equation may be rearranged to obtain

$$\text{(V.15)} \qquad \beta_s^{ITC} - \beta_s^{TX} = \frac{\tau_o - \tau_1}{1-\tau_o}\,(1-e^{-(r+\delta)(t^*-s)})(1-\beta_s^{ITC}) \quad \text{for} \quad t \leq s < t^* .$$

Note that since $\tau_o > \tau_1$ and $1-\beta_s^{ITC} > 0$, β_s^{ITC} exceeds β_s^{TX} for $t \leq s < t^*$. The reason is that P_K is higher under the tax cut than under the investment tax credit because the after-tax rentals are increased during the regime of the tax cut. Thus, investment would be higher under the tax cut than under the investment tax credit if β were the same in both cases. Since β is essentially the present value of the firm's tax bill saving accruing to current investment, raising β^{ITC} relative to β^{TX} raises investment under the investment tax credit policy relative to investment under the tax cut, until it is equal in the two cases. Thus β_s^{ITC} exceeds β_x^{TX}. Note, however, that as we approach the end of the tax cut regime, P_K^{TX} approaches $\frac{(1-\tau_o)\phi^*}{r+\delta}$ so that the required wedge between β_s^{ITC} and β_s^{TX} is reduced.

Now we are ready to compare tax revenues under the two policy alternatives. Since the policies generate identical time paths of investment and output, the tax policies will yield the same tax revenue from t* onward, since the tax regimes become identical at t*. Therefore, we need only compare the difference in tax revenues up to t*. Let R_{t*}^{ITC} be the present value of net corporate tax revenues from t to t*, discounted to time t. Then we obtain

$$\text{(V.16)} \qquad R_{t*}^{ITC} = \tau_o \int_t^{t*} \phi^* K_s e^{-r(s-t)} ds - \int_t^{t*} \beta_s^{ITC}\, c(I_s) e^{-r(s-t)} ds$$

Defining R_{t*}^{TX} similarly for the tax cut policy, we have

$$\text{(V.17)} \qquad R^{TX}_{t*} = \tau_1 \int_t^{t*} \phi^* K_s e^{-r(s-t)} ds - \int_t^{t*} \beta^{TX}_s\, c(I_s) e^{-r(s-t)} ds$$

Subtracting (V.17) from (V.16) and using (V.15) to substitute for $\beta_s^{ITC} - \beta_s^{TX}$ we obtain the following equivalent expressions for the difference in tax revenues under the two policies,

$$\text{(V.18)} \quad \text{a.} \quad R^{ITC}_{t*} - R^{TX}_{t*} = \frac{\tau_o - \tau_1}{1-\tau_o} \int_t^{t*} \{(1-\tau_o)\phi^* K_s - (1-e^{-(r+\delta)(t^*-s)})(1-\beta_s^{ITC})c(I_s)e^{-r(s-t)}\}\, ds$$

$$\text{b.} \quad = \frac{\tau_o - \tau_1}{1-\tau_o} \{ V^{ITC}_{t*} + \int_t^{t*} e^{-(r+\delta)(t^*-s)} (1-\beta_s^{ITC}) c(I_s) e^{-r(s-t)} ds$$

Note that in (V. 8 .b), V^{ITC}_{t*} is defined as the present value of the cash flow of the firm between t and t*.[1]

In order to determine which of the alternative policies yields a greater tax revenue, we must determine the sign of the expression in (V.18). Observe that if V^{ITC}_{t*} were positive, then the investment tax credit would yield more revenue than the tax cut. However, there is no presumption that V^{ITC}_{t*} is positive for finite t*. While it is true that the present value of the cash flow of viable firms is positive, this present value of cash flow refers to the entire (infinite) life of the firm. It is quite possible that if a firm's current capital stock is far below K*, it might be undergoing investment expenditures which

---

[1]This includes the present value of the depreciation allowance on capital installed during this period, although some of the benefit of the depreciation allowance does not accrue to the firm until after t*.

exceed its current operating profit for some time. However, if the firm's capital stock is not too far below K*, and if the magnitude of the stimulus to investment is moderate, then V_{t*}^{ITC} will be positive, and the investment tax credit policy will yield more tax revenue than the tax cut. In the appendix, we present a simple example to illustrate this point. Also in the appendix we present an example in which the firm's capital stock is far below K* and the tax cut yields greater tax revenue than the equivalent investment tax credit policy. To summarize, our discussion of the relative costs to the Treasury of temporary fiscal policies leads only to the soft conclusion that in "reasonable" cases, the investment tax credit is the cheaper policy. By "reasonable" cases, we mean situations in which the firm is not far from the steady state and in which the stimulus to investment is moderate.

VI. Temporary Fiscal Policies in the Fixed Output Case

In this section we compare the corporate tax revenues under a temporary tax cut and a temporary investment tax credit, for the case of an output constrained firm. The analysis of policy in this case is much more cumbersome than in the fixed price case and, not surprisingly, the conclusions of this section are also "soft". However, the analysis of this section is of interest because it develops a general expression for the difference in tax revenues under the two policies. This formula is general in that it applies to all durations, temporary or permanent, and to all demand curves for the firm's output. The limitation of this expression is that its algebraic sign is unambiguous only for permanent policies. As in Section V, there is some ambiguity of sign when the expression is applied to temporary policies.

Let ρ_s be the pre-tax rental to capital at time s. In the fixed output case, $\rho_s = \rho_s(K_s, Q_s, w_s)$, i.e., the rental is a function of the capital stock, the sales constraint, and the wage rate. Now assume that Q_s and w_s are given for $s \geq t$ and we consider a temporary tax cut and the equivalent investment tax credit policy. Equivalent policies lead to the same time path of capital K_s, $s \geq t$, so that $\rho_s^{TX} = \rho_s^{ITC}$ for $s \geq t$. Now we define

$$\text{(VI.1)} \qquad \Delta_{1,t} = \int_t^{t^*} \rho_s e^{-(r+\delta)(s-t)} ds$$

$$\Delta_{2,t} = \int_{t^*}^{\infty} \rho_s e^{-(r+\delta)(s-t)} ds$$

Note that $\Delta_{1,t} + \Delta_{2,t}$ is the present value of the pre-tax rentals accruing to the undepreciated portion of a unit of capital installed at time t. The present value of the rentals accruing during the temporary policy is given by $\Delta_{1,t}$, and the present value of the rentals accruing after the policy ends is given by $\Delta_{2,t}$. Under the temporary tax cut, τ_1 is the corporate tax rate until t*, and τ_o is the corporate tax rate after t*. Therefore,

$$\text{(VI.2)} \qquad P_{K,t}^{TX} = (1-\tau_1)\Delta_{1,t} + (1-\tau_o)\Delta_{2,t} \quad .$$

Under the investment tax credit policy, the corporate tax rate is constant and equal to τ_o so that

$$\text{(VI.3)} \qquad P_{K,t}^{ITC} = (1-\tau_o)(\Delta_{1,t} + \Delta_{2,t})$$

Note that $P_{K,t}^{TX}$ exceeds $P_{K,t}^{ITC}$ by $(\tau_o-\tau_1)\Delta_{1,t}$ so that if the rate of investment is to be the same under both policies, β^{ITC} must be greater than β^{TX}, as explained in Section V. The exact relationship between β_s^{ITC} and β_s^{TX} for all $s < t^*$ may be determined by solving the condition $(P_K^{TX}/(1-\beta^{TX}))_s = (P_K^{ITC}/(1-\beta^{ITC}))_s$ for $s < t^*$. Substituting from (VI.2) and (VI.3) for $P_{K,s}^{TX}$ and $P_{K,s}^{ITC}$, respectively, and solving for $\beta_s^{ITC} - \beta_s^{TX}$, we obtain

$$\text{(VI.4)} \qquad \beta_s^{ITC} - \beta_s^{TX} = \frac{(\tau_o-\tau_1)\Delta_{1,s}}{(1-\tau_o)(\Delta_{1,s}+\Delta_{2,s})} (1 - \beta_s^{ITC}), \quad s \leq t^* .$$

From (VI.4) it is clear that β_s^{ITC} exceeds β_s^{TX}, as expected. Also, as s approaches t*, the gap between β_s^{ITC} and β_s^{TX}, expressed as a proportion of $(1-\beta_s^{ITC})$, narrows toward zero.

We may now compare tax revenues under the two fiscal policies. Since the tax codes as well as the time paths of investment are identical after t*, we need only compare tax revenues accruing up to t*. Recalling that R_{t*}^{ITC} is the present value of tax revenue up to t*, under the temporary investment tax credit, we have

$$\text{(VI.5)} \qquad R_{t*}^{ITC} = \tau_o \int_t^{t*} \pi_s e^{-r(s-t)} ds - \int_t^{t*} \beta_s^{ITC} c(I_s) e^{-r(s-t)} ds$$

where π_s is the operating profit at time s, i.e., $\pi_s = PQ_s - wL_s$. There is an analogous expression for the present value of tax revenues under the tax cut

$$\text{(VI.6)} \qquad R_{t*}^{TX} = \tau_1 \int_t^{t*} \pi_s e^{-r(s-t)} ds - \int_t^{t*} \beta_s^{TX} c(I_s) e^{-r(s-t)} ds .$$

To compare the present value of the tax revenues under the two policies, we subtract (VI.6) from (VI.5), and use (VI.4) to substitute for $\beta_s^{ITC} - \beta_x^{TX}$, to obtain

$$\text{(VI.7)} \qquad R_{t*}^{ITC} - R_{t*}^{TX} = \frac{\tau_o - \tau_1}{1-\tau_o} \{V_{t*}^{ITC} + \int_t^{t*} \frac{\Delta_{2,s}}{\Delta_{1,s} + \Delta_{2,s}} (1-\beta_s^{ITC}) c(I_s) e^{-r(s-t)} ds\}$$

This expression is very similar to (V.18) and the interpretation is the same. If V_{t*}^{ITC} , the present value of the firm's cash flow under the investment tax credit until t*, is greater than zero, then the investment tax credit policy yields greater tax revenues than the equivalent tax cut. If the fiscal stimulus is not too large and if the capital stock is not too far below its steady state value, then this condition will be satisfied.

The expression for $R_{t*}^{ITC} - R_{t*}^{TX}$ in (VI.7) is quite general. It applies to all demand curves, not just the vertical demand curve assumed in the derivation. In general, the rental ρ_s is a function of K_s, w_s and the demand conditions at time s. Our derivation for equivalent fiscal policies remains valid if we assume that w_s and the demand conditions at time s are given for all s, rather than simply assuming that w_s and Q_s are given for all s. Indeed, (VI.7) applies to the case of a price-taking firm facing the same price for all s. In this case, $\frac{\Delta_{2,s}}{\Delta_{1,s}+\Delta_{2,s}} = e^{-(r+\delta)(t*-s)}$ and (VI.7) is identical to (V.18.b). The expression for $R_{t*}^{ITC} - R_{t*}^{TX}$ is also general with respect to the duration of the policies. It applies to permanent policies also, if we let t* be infinite. In this case, $V_{t*}^{ITC} = V^{ITC}$, and $\Delta_{2,s} = 0$ for all s so that (VI.7) is identical to (II.18) and (III.13). To summarize, we have a general expression for the difference in tax revenues under equivalent fiscal policies. This expression applies to all types of demand curves and to all durations of policy. For permanent policies, we have the result that tax revenues are higher under the investment tax credit than under a tax cut. The corresponding result for temporary policies is not as strong. There is merely a presumption that for a moderate stimulus to investment in the neighborhood of steady state, the investment tax credit produces higher tax revenues than the tax cut.

VII. Concluding Remarks

In this essay we have compared the effects of an investment tax credit and a corporate tax cut. Equivalent permanent fiscal policies, which are defined as leading to the same steady state capital stock, are shown to have identical paths to the steady state. However, the tax revenue to the Treasury is greater for an investment tax credit than for a corporate tax cut. The investment tax credit is aimed quite specifically at increasing investment, and it gives a bigger "bang per buck" than a corporate tax cut. Essentially, the investment tax credit increases investment by increasing the after-tax returns to new capital, whereas the corporate tax cut increases the after-tax return to old capital as well as new capital. When we extend the analysis to temporary tax rate changes, we must take into account the time pattern of the depreciation allowance. Without some restrictions on the depreciation allowance schedule, we cannot even determine whether investment increases or decreases in response to a temporary tax cut. By assuming that the depreciation allowance is proportional to physical depreciation, we find that a temporary tax cut increases investment. However, the possibility that a temporary tax cut can have the opposite effect in the presence of accelerated depreciation may be a reason to shy away from a temporary tax cut in favor of a temporary investment tax credit policy. In addition, there is a weak presumption that the investment tax credit policy is less costly to the Treasury than an equivalent tax cut, even when the policies are explicitly temporary.

The analysis of this essay is unabashedly partial equilibrium in nature. Within this model it is not necessary to examine the tax revenue from an income tax on labor income because equivalent fiscal policies have identical effects on income tax revenue from labor income. That is, within the partial equilibrium framework of this paper, there is a complete accounting of net tax revenues derived from taxes on corporate income and labor income, so that our conclusions about the relative costs of alternative policies continue to hold even when we consider the personal income tax.

APPENDIX

I. The "Reasonable Case"

In this section of the Appendix we examine the effect of moderate fiscal policies on a price-taking firm. Suppose that the firm is initially in the steady state and that the investment cost function is $c(I) = aI^2$. Since $c'(I^*) = \frac{P_K}{(1-\beta)}$, where $I^* = \delta K^*$ is steady state investment, and $1-\beta^o$ is $1-k_o - \tau_o z$, we have

$$\text{(A.I.1)} \qquad I^* = \frac{1}{2a} \frac{(1-\tau_o)\phi^*}{(r+\delta)} \frac{1}{1-\beta^o}$$

The cash flow per unit time in the steady state, F, is equal to the operating profit, $(1-\tau_o)\phi^* K^*$, less net capital expenditure, $(1-\beta^o)c(I)$, so that

$$\text{(A.I.2)} \qquad F = (1-\tau_o)\phi^* K^* \{1- \frac{\delta}{2(\tau+\delta)}\}$$

Note that the net cash outflow associated with capital expenditures is less than one half of the operating profit.

Now consider an increase in the investment tax credit which is equivalent to a temporary tax cut as discussed in Section V. This policy leaves P_K unchanged but reduces $1-\beta$ to $1-\beta^{ITC}$. Therefore, $\frac{P_K}{(1-\beta)}$ rises to $\frac{P_K}{(1-\beta^{ITC})} = \frac{1-\beta^o}{1-\beta^{ITC}} \frac{P_K}{1-\beta^o}$, I rises to $(1-\beta^o)/(1-\beta^{ITC}))\ I^*$ and $c(I)$ rises to $((1-\beta^o)/(1-\beta^{ITC}))^2 c(I^*)$. Hence,

$$(A.I.3) \quad (1-\beta^{ITC})c(I) = \frac{1-\beta^{o}}{1-\beta^{ITC}}(1-\beta^{o})c(I^*) .$$

Since the policy increases the rate of investment, $K_s \geq K^*$ for all $s \geq t$, with strict inequality holding for at least some s. Therefore, using (V.18) and observing that $\int_t^{t^*}(1-\beta_s^{ITC})e^{-(r+\delta)(t^*-s)}c(I_s)e^{-r(s-t)}ds > 0$,

we obtain

$$(A.I.4) \quad R_{t^*}^{ITC} - R_{t^*}^{TX} > \frac{\tau_o-\tau_1}{1-\tau_o}\int_t^{t^*}\{(1-\tau_o)\phi^*K^* - (\frac{1-\beta^{o}}{1-\beta_s^{ITC}})(1-\beta^{o})c(I^*)\}e^{-r(s-t)}ds .$$

Recall from Section V that $\frac{P_K}{(1-\beta_s^{ITC})}$ falls over time so that $\frac{(1-\beta^{o})}{(1-\beta_s^{ITC})}$

also falls over time. If we assume that the initial stimulus to investment increases investment by less than a factor of two, i.e.,

$\frac{(1-\beta^{o})}{(1-\beta_t^{ITC})} < 2$, then

$$(A.I.5) \quad \frac{1-\beta^{o}}{1-\beta_s^{ITC}} < 2 \quad \text{for} \quad t \leq s < t^* .$$

Combining expressions (A.I.4) and (A.I.5), we obtain

$$(A.I.6) \quad R_{t^*}^{ITC} - R_{t^*}^{TX} > \frac{\tau_o-\tau_1}{1-\tau_o}\int_t^{t^*}\{(1-\tau_o)\phi^*K^* - 2(1-\beta^{o})c(I^*)\}e^{-r(s-t)}ds .$$

Substituting (A.I.1) into (A.I.6) and using the fact that $c(I) = aI^2$, we obtain

$$(A.I.7) \quad R_{t^*}^{ITC} - R_{t^*}^{TX} > (\tau_o-\tau_1)\int_t^{t^*}\phi^*K^*(1 - \frac{\delta}{r+\delta})e^{-r(s-t)}ds > 0 ,$$

Hence, the tax revenue is greater under the investment tax credit policy than under the tax cut. This derivation would also apply if the initial capital stock were greater than K*. If K_t were less than K*, the derivation could be modified to show that $R_{t*}^{ITC} > R_{t*}^{TX}$ for K_t sufficiently close to K*.

II. The "Perverse Case"

In this section we construct a case in which the tax revenues under the investment tax credit are less than under the tax cut. Assume that the capital stock is far below the steady state level so that even at the end of the temporary fiscal policy

$$(A.II.1)\quad K_{t*} = K^* \frac{1-e^{-\delta(t*-t)}}{4} < K^*$$ [1]

For simplicity we let $r = \delta$.

Before the temporary policy begins, investment equals the level of steady state replacement investment and is given by (A.I.1). While the stimulus policy is in effect, investment is higher than this level. The value of $(1-\beta_s^{ITC})c(I_s)$ for $t \leq s < t*$ is given by (A.I.3). Now we wish to determine the algebraic sign of

$$(A.II.2)\quad R_{t*}^{ITC} - R_{t*}^{TX} = \frac{\tau_o - \tau_1}{1-\tau_o} \int_t^{t*} \{(1-\tau_o)\phi^* K_s e^{-r(s-t)} - (1-e^{-(r+\delta)(t*-s)})(1-\beta_s^{ITC})c(I_s)e^{-r(s-t)}\}ds$$

---

[1]Even though K_t << K* and the firm may have substantial negative cash flow for a while, our assumption that V, the present value of the cash flow, be positive is not violated. [Footnote continued on next page.]

Since $K_s < K_{t*}$ for $s < t*$ and $(1-\beta_s^{ITC})c(I_s) = \frac{1-\beta^o}{1-\beta_s^{ITC}} a(1-\beta^o)(\delta K*)^2 >$

$a(1-\beta^o)(\delta K*)^2$ for $s < t*$, we obtain

$$(A.II.3) \quad R_{t*}^{ITC} - R_{t*}^{TX} < \frac{\tau_o - \tau_1}{1-\tau_o} \int_t^{t*} \{(1-\tau_o)\phi^* K_{t*} - (1-e^{-(r+\delta)(t*-s)}) a(1-\beta^o)(\delta K*)^2\} e^{-r(s-t)} ds \ .$$

Simplifying (A.II.3) and using the fact that $r = \delta$, we obtain

$$(A.II.4) \quad R_{t*}^{ITC} - R_{t*}^{TX} < \frac{\tau_o - \tau_1}{1-\tau_o} \frac{1-e^{-\delta(t*-t)}}{\delta} \{(1-\tau_o)\phi^* K_{t*} - a(1-\beta^o)(\delta K*)^2 (1-e^{-\delta(t*-t)})\} \ .$$

Using (A.II.1) to substitute for K_{t*} and (A.I.1) to substitute for $\delta K*$, the term in brackets can be shown to be equal to zero. Therefore,

$$(A.II.5) \quad R_{t*}^{ITC} - R_{t*}^{TX} < 0$$

so that the tax revenue under the investment tax credit is less than under the tax cut.

[Footnote continued from previous page.]
It can be shown that $V = \frac{(1-\tau_o)\phi^*}{r(r+\sigma)} (\frac{1}{2} \delta K^* + rK_t)$, if there is total carry forward of tax losses with full discounting. Therefore, $K_t > 0$ guarantees that V will be positive.

ESSAY IV

LIMITED *EX POST* SUBSTITUTABILITY AND OPTIMAL VARIATIONS IN CAPACITY UTILIZATION

I. Introduction

In neoclassical studies of production and investment behavior, the distinction between ex ante and ex post factor substitutability is generally ignored in favor of a putty-putty production function. Although these studies treat the capital stock as fixed at a point of time, capital is assumed to be perfectly malleable. Not only can the existing capital stock be used in combination with almost any amount of variable input, but, in addition, nothing is lost relative to the ex ante production function by changing the labor capital ratio on existing capital. That is, for a putty-putty production function, the ex ante isoquants are identical to the ex post isoquants. One feature of the putty-putty model is that a cost minimizing firm will never have idle capital. If there were some unused capital, then the firm could reduce total variable costs by substituting capital for the variable inputs. Hence, a putty-putty model of production with fixed capital and freely adjustable variable inputs is not capable of explaining variations in capacity utilization within an optimizing framework.

An alternative to the conventional putty-putty model is the putty-clay model. In the putty-clay model, once capital is installed in place it becomes less malleable. In the extreme case, the labor capital ratio cannot ever be varied on existing installed capital. In less extreme cases, the labor capital ratio can be changed on existing capital, but the new combination of labor and existing capital will produce less output than if the same combination of labor and newly installed capital were used. Essentially, the ex post elasticity of substitution of capital for variable inputs is lower than the corresponding ex ante elasticity of substitution. That is, there is limited ex post factor substitutability.

This paper examines the optimal dynamic behavior of a firm with a production function characterized by limited ex post factor substitutability. The firm's ex ante prduction function is Cobb-Douglass, but the ex post production function is a fixed coefficients production function. Thus, the elasticity of substitution of the two factors, labor and capital, falls from an ex ante value of unity to an ex post value of zero. Analytically, this feature is achieved by treating labor as a quasi-fixed factor, as in Nadiri and Rosen (1969). Since at any point of time, labor and capital are fixed, the firm's current production decision is limited to choosing the optimal rates of utilization of these quasi-fixed factors. By constraining the rates of utilization to be the same for the two factors, the ex post production function becomes a fixed coefficients production function, at a given point of time. Within the framework of this model, we can examine the determinants of optimal capacity utilization.

The dynamic framework of this paper is similar to that in Abel (1978a) in which a very neoclassical version of Tobin's q approach to investment is derived from explicit dynamic optimization of the firm. In that paper, investment was shown to be an increasing function of the shadow price of installed capital goods, divided by the tax-adjusted price of uninstalled capital goods. This investment equation also applies to the model of this paper. Indeed, the analysis of this paper generalizes this type of investment equation to any quasi-fixed factor pf production. Investment in labor, which is a quasi-fixed factor, is shown to be an increasing function of the shadow price of the existing stock of labor on the firm's payroll; clearly, this is analogous to the q approach to investment in capital goods. In general, the firm's investment decision in each quasi-fixed factor is determined by the shadow price of that factor. Within the perfect foresight model of this paper, we can examine the dynamic path of investment.[1] By analyzing the forward-looking investment decision together with the static production decision, we can examine the relation between investment and capacity utilization.

In Section II, we set up the model and solve a simple static optimization problem which will help with the interpretation of the results in later sections. In Section III, we solve the firm's dynamic optimization problem to determine the rates of investment in the quasi-fixed factors and the rate of capacity utilization. We develop a graphical apparatus to characterize the steady state in Section IV and use this apparatus in section V to analyze comparative steady states. In Section VI, we analyze the dynamic properties of our system and determine the stable path to the steady state. This stable path is used in Section VII to analyze the dynamic behavior of capacity utilization and its relation to investment in capital. In Section VIII, we introduce corporate taxes, the depreciation allowance, and the investment tax credit into the analysis. Finally, in Section IX, we present concluding remarks.

---

[1]The putty-clay model also has implications for the relative dynamic responses of investment to an increase in output demand and a decrease in the cost of capital, as shown by Bischoff (1971). We do not examine this issue here. See Essay I, Section VII, for a demonstration that the response patterns predicted by Bischoff can be obtained from a model with a putty-putty production function.

II. The Model

The Production Function

We assume that the firm's ex ante production function is Cobb-Douglas in its two factors, labor services, L*, and capital services, K*, so that $X_t = L_t^{*\alpha} K_t^{*1-\alpha}$, where X_t is output at time t. At any point of time the firm has a stock of physical capital K and a stock of labor L. The stock of labor is the roster of employees on the firm's payroll. Labor services are proportional to the stock of labor so that $L^* = \beta L$. Similarly, for capital services, we have $K^* = \gamma K$. Hence the production function may be written in terms of the stocks of labor and capital and the utilization rates as $X = (\beta L)^{\alpha}(\gamma K)^{1-\alpha}$, with the appropriate choice of units.[1] We make the further assumption that $\beta=\gamma$, i.e., that the stocks of labor and capital are used to the same degree of intensity. This is a very reasonable formulation in the short run. In order to use a machine more intensively, it is operated for more hours per day. The longer working day of a machine requires that the working day of labor be increased, i.e., that labor is used more intensively. Under the assumption that $\beta= \gamma$, the production function is $X = \beta L^{\alpha}K^{1-\alpha}$. In the sort run, β is a decision variable, but L and K are fixed.[2] Thus, at any point of time, there is a fixed coefficients production function with the ratio of labor services to capital services determined by the inherited stocks of labor and capital. As time passes, the stocks of

---

[1]This production function is of the type presented by Nadiri and Rosen (1969) in which we impose the restriction that the elasticity of output with respect to the stock of a given factor equals the elasticity of output with respect to the utilization of that factor.

[2]In the Nadiri-Rosen framework, we have assumed that the utilization rate may be instantaneously adjusted to its desired value at every point of time. Nadiri and Rosen agree that "certainly there is some intuitive sense to this view," although they do not adopt this assumption.

labor and capital can be varied at some cost. Hence, the labor services/ capital services ratio can vary over time.

The Wage Function

Let $w(\beta)$ be the total wages paid to each employee on the firm's payroll. The utilization rate β is essentially an index of hours worked per employee. Let $w^*(\beta)$ be the hourly wage rate so that $w(\beta) = w(\beta)\beta$. In an attempt to model overtime pay, we assume that the hourly wage rate increases with the number of hours worked per unit of time, i.e., that $w^{*\prime}(\beta) \geq 0$. Therefore, $w'(\beta) \geq 0$ and $w''(\beta) \geq 0$ for $\beta \geq 0$, with strict inequality for $\beta > 0$. That is, $w(\beta)$ is an increasing convex function of β.[1] For simplicity, we assume that $w(\beta)$ is quadratic in β

$$\text{(II.1)} \qquad w(\beta) = w(a_o\beta^2 + a_1\beta + a_2) \qquad\qquad a_o > 0,\ a_1 > 0.$$

The restrictions that a_o and a_1 be positive are required so that $w(\beta)$ satisfies the assumed convexity and positive marginal wage conditions. In addition, it seems reasonable to assume that $a_2 > 0$ to prevent $w(\beta)$ from being negative when labor utilization is zero.

In order to examine the effects of this nonlinear wage function in a more conventional framework, we solve a static optimization problem, in which labor can be costlessly and instantaneously adjusted. The firm has a fixed stock of capital and can sell its output at the fixed price P. We assume that the firm chooses L and β to maximize its current profit, $\pi = P\beta L^{\alpha}K^{1-\alpha} - w(\beta)L$. The first order conditions for this problem are

[1] If the hourly wage rate were invariant to hours worked, then $w(\beta)$ would be a linear function of β and the optimal value of β would be indeterminate, when labor is treated as a quasi-fixed factor as in Section III and following.

$$\text{(II.2)}\quad \text{a.}\quad \frac{\partial \pi}{\partial L} = \alpha P\beta L^{\alpha-1}K^{1-\alpha} - w(\beta) = 0$$

$$\text{b.}\quad \frac{\partial \pi}{\partial \beta} = PL^{\alpha}K^{1-\alpha} - w'(\beta)L = 0,$$

from which we derive $\frac{w'(\beta)}{w(\beta)}\beta = 1/\alpha$. Thus, the optimal value of β is such that the elasticity of $w(\beta)$ with respect to β is $1/\alpha$. Since $\alpha < 1$,[1] the optimal value of β lies on an elastic portion of the $w(\beta)$ curve.[2] The condition that the elasticity of $w(\beta)$ with respect to β equals $1/\alpha$ (along with the second order condition discussed below) determines the optimal β , say β^*. Given β^*, the labor input is chosen so as to set L/K equal to $(w(\beta^*)/\alpha P\beta^*)^{1/(\alpha-1)} = (w'(\beta^*)/P)^{1/(\alpha-1)}$.

The second order condition for this problem will help in the interpretation of the solution of the dynamic optimization problem in later sections. The second order condition for a maximum is that the Hessian be negative definite. That is,

$$\text{(II.3)}\quad \begin{bmatrix} \alpha(\alpha-1)P\beta L^{\alpha-2}K^{1-\alpha} & \alpha PL^{\alpha-1}K^{1-\alpha} - w'(\beta) \\ \alpha PL^{\alpha-1}K^{1-\alpha} - w'(\beta) & -w''(\beta)L \end{bmatrix}$$

must be negative definite. Clearly, the diagonal elements of this matrix are negative, as required. We also require that the determinant of the matrix in (II.3) be positive. This requirement will be satisfied if and only if

---

[1]In this paper we assume that the elasticity of output with respect to labor, α , is greater than the corresponding elasticity for capital, $1-\alpha$. In addition, we make the usual assumption that both elasticities are positive so that $1/2 < \alpha < 1$. This is empirically true for the aggregate production function of the United States.

[2]If the firm's β were on an inelastic portion of $w(\beta)$, an increase in β would increase revenue proportionately but would increase $w(\beta)$ less than proportionately, for given L and K. Since revenue exceeds the wage bill, the increase in β would increase revenue more than it increases the wage bill. Hence, the original β could not have been profit maximizing.

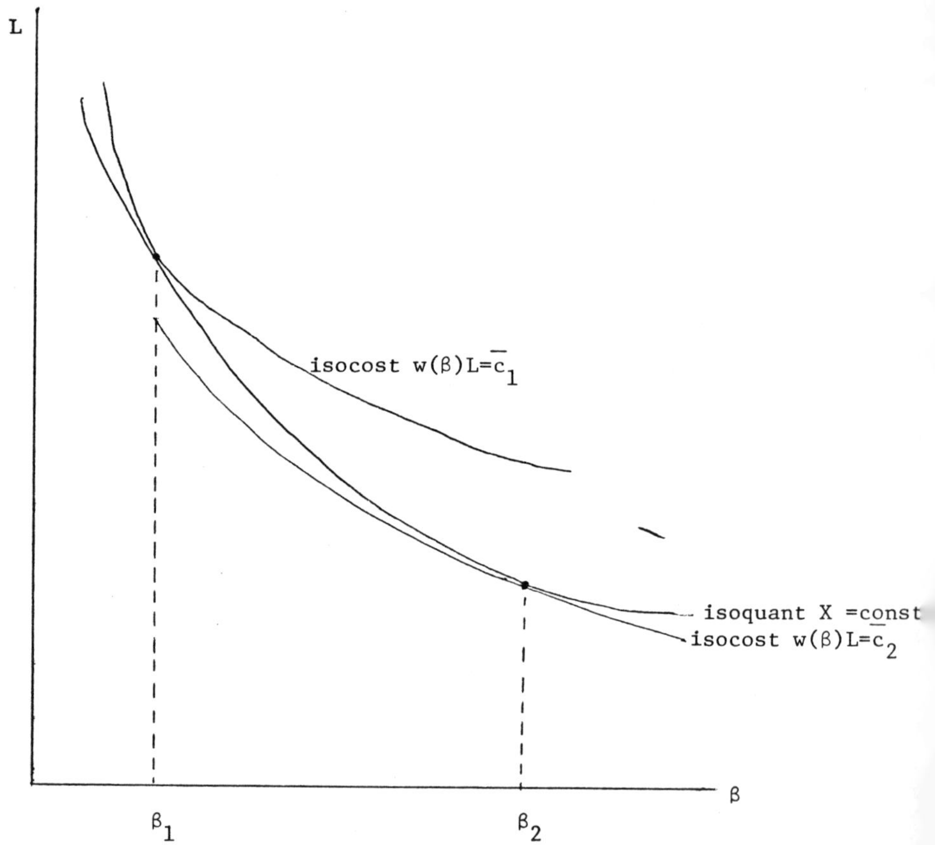

Figure 1

$$(II.4) \quad A = 2a_o(2\alpha-1)\beta + a_1(\alpha-1) > 0.$$

The relevance of the condition that A be positive is illustrated in Figure 1. This diagram shows two isocost curves and one isoquant drawn in β,L space, for given K. The first order conditions are satisfied at both β_1 and β_2. However, only at β_2, corresponding to the higher value of β and the lower value of L, is the second order condition, $A > 0$, satisfied. Thus, the condition that A be positive allows us to choose the optimal β from the values at which the first order condition is satisfied. This condition will be of importance in the dynamic optimization problem, to which we now turn.[1]

III. The Dynamic Optimization Problem

The firm is assumed to maximize the present value of the net cash flow accruing to it over the infinite future. As discussed in section II, the production function of the firm is $X = \beta L^{\alpha}K^{1-\alpha}$. The utilization factor β is a decision variable at every point of time. The stocks of labor and capital are state variables which can be varied across time by incurring some installation or adjustment cost. We assume that the per unit cost of purchasing and installing capital in place is an increasing convex function of the investment/capital ratio, $c(I/K)$, with $c(0) = 0$, $c'(0) = 0$, $c'(x) > 0$ for $x > 0$, and $c''(x) \geq 0$ for $x \geq 0$.[2] Therefore, the cost of

[1]For the dynamic version of this simple model, in which labor is a costlessly adjustable input, optimal capacity utilization will be constant over time at β^*, if the exogenous variables P and w are constant. Also, the labor capital ratio is always equal to $(w'(\beta^*)/P)^{1/(\alpha-1)}$. See Essay III. The role of labor adjustment costs in the subsequent sections is to introduce the possibility of optimal variations in capacity utilization.

[2]We assume that per unit installation costs are a function of the investment/capital ratio, rather than simply the rate of investment, so that L/K will be a state variable. This will become clear later in this section. Note that this is a very reasonable formulation in the context of growth models. See Essay I.

maintaining a rate of investment I for a time interval dt is Ic(I/K)dt. Analogously, there is an adjustment cost function associated with changing the size of the firm's labor force. The gross rate of change of L is denoted by I_L, and per unit adjustment costs are an increasing function of I_L/L, which we write as $D(I_L/L)$. We assume that $D(0) = 0$, $D'(0) = 0$, $D'(x) > 0$ for $x > 0$ and $D''(x) \geq 0$ for $x \geq 0$.[1] Therefore, the cost of maintaining a rate of labor investment I_L for a time interval dt is $I_L D(I_L/L)dt$. The two rates of investment, I and I_L, are also decision varaibles of the firm. Finally we assume that the wage paid to each unit of labor is a quadratic function of the utilization factor β so that $w(\beta) = w(a_o\beta^2 + a_1\beta + a_2)$, with a_o, a_1, and a_2 greater than zero, as discussed in section II. The variable w may viewed as the scale wage and the quadratic function in β embodies the overtime wage function . The wage cost at any point of time is thus $w(a_o\beta^2 + a_1\beta + a_2)L$. The firm's optimization problem is to choose β, I, and I_L to maximize V, the present value of its cash flow:

$$\text{(III.1)} \quad \max_{\beta, I, I_L} V = \int_o^\infty \{P\beta L_t^\alpha K_t^{1-\alpha} - w(a_o\beta^2 + a_1\beta + a_2)L - Ic(I/K) - I_L D(I_L/L)\}\, e^{-rt} dt,$$

subject to $\dot{K} = I - \delta K$ and $\dot{L} = I_L - \mu L$, where δ is the depreciation rate of the capital stock and μ is the depreciation rate of the labor stock.

The optimization problem may be solved using the maximum principle of Pontryagin. The Hamiltonian for this problem is

$$\text{(III.2)} \quad H = \{P\beta L^\alpha K^{1-\alpha} - w(a_0\beta^2 + a_1\beta + a_2)L - Ic(I/K) - I_L D(I_L/L)\}\, e^{-rt} + P_K e^{-rt}(I - \delta K) + P_L e^{-rt}(I_L - \mu L),$$

where P_K and P_L are the shadow prices of capital and labor, respectively. The first step in the solution process is to take the partial derivatives

[1] We have assumed that the adjustment cost function is separable in the two gross rates of growth of the quasi-fixed factors. If the adjustment costs are internal to the firm, the assumption would require further justification. However, if the adjustment costs are external to the firm, then separability is a very reasonable assumption. One justification for this separability of the adjustment cost function is that the firm faces upward-sloping flow supply curves in the markets for each of the two quasi-fixed factors, and that the supply curves for these two factors have no significant interrelationships.

of the Hamiltonian with respect to each of the three decision variables and to set each of these partial derivatives equal to zero. The partial of H with respect to β is

(III.3) $\frac{\partial H}{\partial \beta} = e^{-rt}\{PL^{\alpha}K^{1-\alpha} - wL(2a_o\beta + a_1)\}$.

Setting this expression equal to zero and solving for β we obtain

(III.4) $\beta = (1/2a_o) \{ \frac{P}{w} (\frac{L}{K})^{\alpha-1} - a_1\}$.[1]

Note that β is a decreasing function of the real scale wage w/P so that the firm desires to use its factors more intensively and incur a greater overtime charge when the real scale wage is lower. Observe that the optimal β is a decreasing function of the labor/capital ratio. This relationship may be illustrated by considering an increase in K, holding L constant, which, of course, reduces L/K. This increase in K increases the marginal revenue product of β, $PL^{\alpha}K^{1-\alpha}$. However, the increase in K does not affect the short run marginal cost schedule, written as a function of β, $wL(wa_o\beta + a_1)$. Therefore, marginal revenue equals marginal cost at a higher level of β. Hence, the increase in K leads to a higher optimal β but a lower labor/capital ratio.

Now we differentiate H with respect to I to obtain

(III.5) $\frac{\partial H}{\partial I} = e^{-rt}\{-c(I/K) - (I/K)c'(I/K) + P_K\}$.

It is convenient to define $c^*(I/K) = c(I/K) + (I/K)c'(I/K)$, which is the marginal cost of increasing the rate of investment, given the level of the capital stock K. Setting $\frac{\partial H}{\partial I}$ equal to zero, we obtain

(III.6) $I/K = c^{*-1}(P_K)$.

Since $c^{*\prime}(\ ) > 0$, we have that the investment/capital ratio is an increasing

[1]Since $a_1 > 0$, β might be negative. To avoid this situation, we assume that a_1 is less than the minimum value of $(P/w)(L/K)^{\alpha-1}$. If no such positive bound exists, we could require that a_1 equal zero, without losing anything from our analysis.

function of P_K, the shadow price of installed capital goods. This is equivalent to the q approach of Tobin, as explained in Abel (1978a).

In an analogous manner, we set $\partial H/\partial I_L$ equal to zero to obtain

$$(III.7) \quad I_L/L = D^{*\prime -1}(P_L),$$

where $D^*(I_L/L) = D(I_L/L) + (I_L/L)D'(I_L/L)$. Hence, the growth rate of the labor stock is an increasing function of the shadow price of labor.

IV. The Steady State Solution

Now that we have determined the optimal values of the decision variables at each point of time, we can study the steady state of the system. The steady state is characterized by a constant value for the utilization factor β and constant values for the growth rates of the stocks of labor and capital. From (III.4), we observe that an implication of the constant value of optimal β, given that the real scale wage w/P is constant, is that the labor capital ratio is constant. An implication of the constant growth rate of capital is that P_K is constant, since the growth rate of capital is a function solely of P_K. Similarly, a constant value for the growth rate of labor implies that P_L is constnat. Therefore, an alternative characterization of the steady state is that L/K, P_K, and P_L are all constant. We shall use this characterization of the steady state in the graphical analysis below. We proceed by first analyzing the following loci: $\dot{L/K} = 0$, $\dot{P}_K = 0$, and $\dot{P}_L = 0$. The steady state is then determined by the intersection of these three loci with the aid of a four-quadrant diagram.

The $\dot{L/K} = 0$ Locus

We may determine how the labor/capital ratio evolves over time by taking the derivative of L/K with respect to time to obtain $\dot{L/K} = (L/K)(\dot{L}/L - \dot{K}/$

Now substitute $I_L/L - \mu$ for $\dot{L}/L$ and $I/K - \delta$ for $\dot{K}/K$ to obtain

(IV.1) $\dot{L/K} = (L/K)\,(I_L/L - I/K - \mu + \delta\,).$

The time rate of change of the labor/capital ratio is a function of only the costate variables P_K and P_L and the labor/capital ratio itself. Note that the algebraic sign of $\dot{L/K}$ is independent of the value of L/K (so long as L/K > 0). Hence, the $\dot{L/K} = 0$ locus may be drawn in P_L, P_K space and is invariant with respect to changes in L/K. To determine the slope of this locus, we observe that $\frac{\partial \dot{L/K}}{\partial P_K} = -\frac{L}{K}\frac{1}{c^{*\prime}} < 0$ and $\frac{\partial \dot{L/K}}{\partial P_L} = \frac{L}{K}\frac{1}{D^{*\prime}} > 0$, so that $\left.\frac{dP_K}{dP_L}\right|_{\dot{L/K}=0} = -\frac{\partial(\dot{L/K})/P_L}{\partial(\dot{L/K})/P_K} > 0$. Essentially, to satisfy $\dot{L/K} = 0$ requires that L and K grow at the same rate. Observe that a higher value for P_L implies a higher growth rate for labor. This higher growth rate of labor requires a higher P_K to call forth the correspondingly higher growth rate of capital. Hence, the $\dot{L/K} = 0$ locus is upward sloping in P_L,P_K space, as shown in figure 2. Also note that for points above the $\dot{L/K} = 0$ locus, P_K is too high relative to P_L so that capital is growing more rapidly than is labor. Hence, $\dot{L/K} < 0$ for points above the $\dot{L/K} = 0$ locus. Conversely, for points below this locus, $\dot{L/K} > 0$.

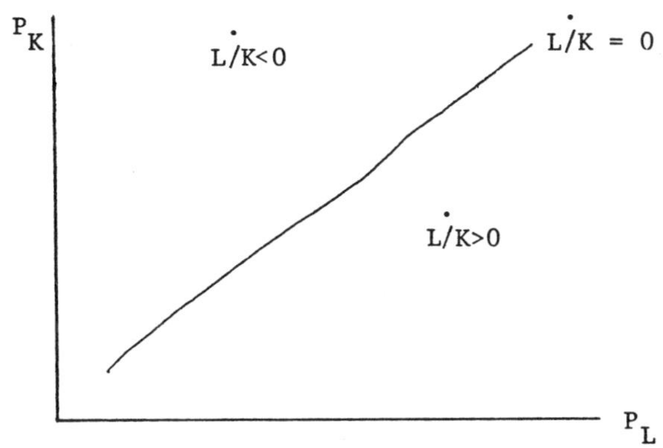

Figure 2

The $\dot{P}_K = 0$ Locus

The time path of P_K may be determined by examining the following necessary condition for an optimum: $\frac{d}{dt}(P_K e^{-rt}) = \frac{-\partial H}{\partial K}$. Taking the indicated derivatives, we obtain

$$\text{(IV.2)} \qquad \dot{P}_K = (r+\delta)P_K - (I/K)^2 c'(I/K) - (1-\alpha)P\beta(L/K)^\alpha ,$$

which may be rewritten as

$$\text{(IV.3)} \qquad (r+\delta)P_K = (1-\alpha)P\beta(L/K)^\alpha + (I/K)^2 c'(I/K) + \dot{P}_K$$

The required rate of return per unit of installed capital appears on the left and is equal to the realized rate of return which appears on the right. The realized return is composed of three parts: the marginal revenue product of a unit of capital; the installation cost saving associated with the reduction in I/K made possible by an extra unit of capital; and the capital gain per unit of capital.

Note the $\dot{P}_K$ is unaffected by P_L so that the $\dot{P}_K = 0$ locus may be drawn in P_K, L/K space. To determine the slope of this locus we must calculate $\partial\dot{P}_K/\partial P_K$ and $\partial \dot{P}_K/\partial(L/K)$. Observe that

$$\text{(IV.4)} \qquad \frac{\partial \dot{P}_K}{\partial P_K} = (r+\delta) - \{2\frac{I}{K}\, c'(\frac{I}{K}) + (\frac{I}{K})^2 c''(\frac{I}{K})\} \; \frac{d(I/K)}{dP_K} .$$

Since $\frac{d(I/K)}{dP_K} = \frac{1}{c^{*\prime}} = \frac{1}{2c'(I/K) + (I/K)c''(I/K)}$, we obtain

$$\text{(IV.5)} \qquad \frac{\partial \dot{P}_K}{\partial P_K} = r + \delta - I/K.$$

In the neighborhood of steady state equilibrium, this partial derivative is positive, since the rate of growth of the capital stock, I/K − δ, must be less than the discount rate, r, for the value V in (III.1) to be finite. Thus an increase in P_K raises the required return on a unit of capital more than it raises the realized return through the installation cost savings. Therefore, $\dot{P}_K$ must increase to bring the realized return up to the required return.

Now we determine the effect of L/K on $\dot{P}_K$. Differentiating $\dot{P}_K$ with respect to L/K, we obtain

$$\text{(IV.6)} \quad \frac{\partial \dot{P}_K}{\partial (L/K)} = -(1-\alpha)P(\frac{L}{K})^{\alpha} \frac{d\beta}{d(L/K)} - \alpha(1-\alpha)P\beta(\frac{L}{K})^{\alpha-1}.$$

Substituting $d\beta/d(L/K) = \frac{\alpha-1}{2a_o} \frac{P}{w} (L/K)^{\alpha-2}$ into the above expression and simplifying we obtain

$$\text{(IV.7)} \quad \frac{\partial \dot{P}_K}{\partial (L/K)} = \frac{-(1-\alpha)}{2a_o} P (L/K)^{\alpha-1}A,$$

where, as in section II, $A=2a_o(2\alpha-1)\beta + a_1(\alpha-1)$. There is a presumption that A is positive so that $\partial \dot{P}_K/\partial(L/K)$ is negative. In economic terms, an increase in the labor/capital ratio increases the marginal revenue product of capital, which is one component of the realized return in (IV.3). Therefore, the capital gain term is reduced to maintain equality between required and realized rates of return.

Since $\partial \dot{P}_K/\partial P_K$ is positive and $\partial \dot{P}_K/\partial(L/K)$ is negative, the $\dot{P}_K = 0$ locus is upward sloping in P_K, L/K space, as shown in Figure 3.[1] Intuitively, if P_K increases, the required return would effect the realized return.

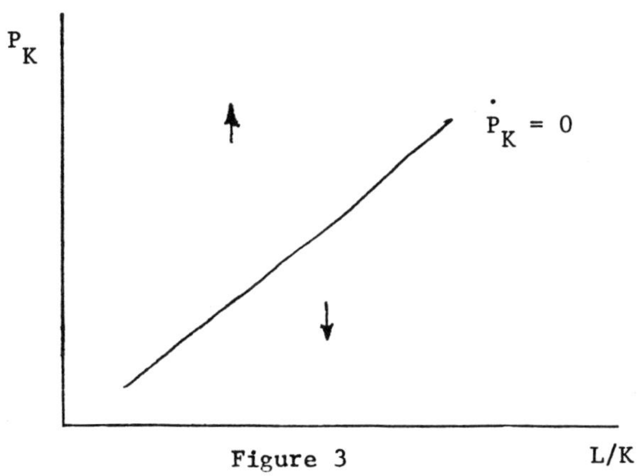

Figure 3

[1]We ignore values of P_K which are high enough to make $r + \delta - (I/K)$ negative.

In order to bring the realized return up to the required return, while maintaining $\dot{P}_K$ equal to zero, L/K must increase. Hence, the $\dot{P}_K$=0 locus slopes upward. Also note that for points above the $\dot{P}_K = 0$ locus, the required return exceeds the realized return, if $\dot{P}_K$ remains equal to zero. Therefore, $\dot{P}_K$ must be positive to bring the realized return up to the required return. Conversely, for points below the $\dot{P}_K = 0$ locus, $\dot{P}_K < 0$.

The $\dot{P}_L = 0$ Locus

The analysis of the time path of P_L is analogous to that for P_K. From the necessary condition for an optimum, $d(P_L e^{-rt})/dt = -\partial H/\partial L$, we obtain

(IV.8) $\dot{P}_L = (r+\mu)P_L - (\frac{I_L}{L})^2 D'(\frac{I_L}{L}) - w(a_o\beta^2(2\alpha-1) + a_1\beta(\alpha-1) - a_2)$,

which may be rewritten as

(IV.9) $(r+\mu)P_L = w(a_o\beta^2(2\alpha-1)+a_1\beta(\alpha-1)-a_2) + (\frac{I_L}{L})^2 D'(\frac{I_L}{L}) + \dot{P}_L$.

The interpretation of this condition is the same as for physical capital where we recognize that $w(a_o\beta^2(2\alpha-1)+a_1\beta(\alpha-1)-a_2)$ is the net marginal revenue product of a unit increase in the labor stock. That is, in equilibrium, the required rate of return equals the sum of the three components of realized return: the marginal revenue product of labor; the installation cost saving due to an extra unit of installed labor; and the capital gain.

Note that $\dot{P}_L$ is independent of P_K so that the $\dot{P}_L = 0$ locus may be drawn in P_L, L/K space. To determine the slope of this locus, we consider an increase in P_L. A higher P_L increases the required return on labor more than it increases the realized return through higher adjustment cost savings. Hence, L/K must fall to bring the realized return up to the required return, while maintaining $\dot{P}_L$ equal to zero. Hence, the $\dot{P}_L = 0$ locus is downward sloping as shown in Figure 4.[1] Note that for points above the $\dot{P}_L = 0$ locus, the required return on labor exceeds the realized return so that $\dot{P}_L$ must be positive to bring the realized return up to the required return. Conversely, for points below the $\dot{P}_L = 0$ locus, $\dot{P}_L$ is negative.

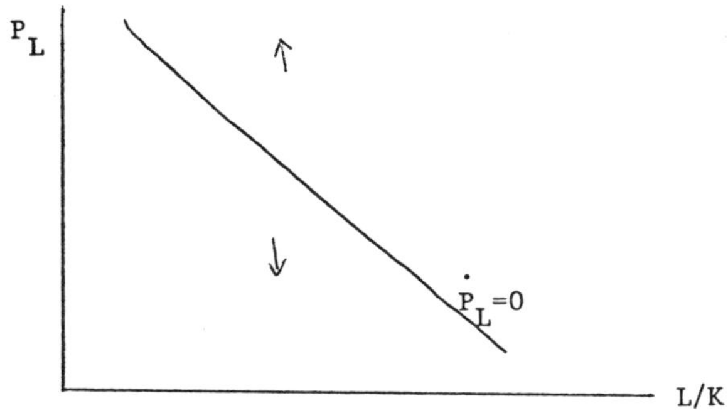

Figure 4

The Four-Quadrant Diagram

Now that we have determined the three loci for which $\dot{L/K} = 0$, $\dot{P}_K = 0$, and $\dot{P}_L = 0$, we examine the steady state solution by finding the point in P_K, P_L, L/K space which lies on all three schedules. An analytic solution of the steady state would be too unwieldy to be of much use, so we present a graphical solution. The graphical solution is facilitated by the fact that each of the loci, $\dot{P}_K=0$, $\dot{P}_L=0$, and $\dot{L/K}=0$, can be drawn in a plane which is orthogonal to one of the three coordinate axes in P_K, P_L, L/K space. We combine these three loci into a four-quadrant diagram which yields the steady state solution graphically. Quadrants I,II and IV correspond to Figure 2, 3, and 4, respectively. In quadrant

---

[1]Formally, we determine that the slope is negative since $\partial\dot{P}_L/\partial P_L = r + \mu - (\dot{I}_L/L)$, which is positive in the neighborhood of the steady state. Also, $\partial\dot{P}_L/\partial(L/K) = ((1-\alpha)/2a_0)P(L/K)^{\alpha-2}A$, which is positive since A is presumed to be positive. Therefore, $\left.\frac{dP_L}{d(L/K)}\right|_{\dot{P}_L=0} < 0$.

III is a 45° line which represents the identity of the variables on the vertical and horizontal axes. The steady state solution is determined by the unique rectangle which has its vertices on the curves in each of the four quadrants, as shown in Figure 5.

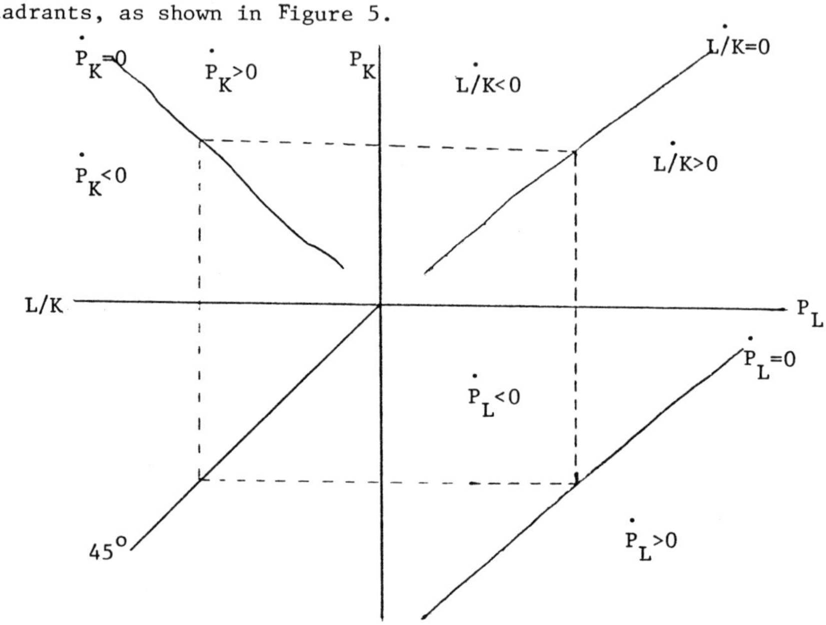

Figure 5

V. Comparative Steady States

The four-quadrant diagram can be used to study comparative steady states. For example, consider an increase in the discount rate r. The increase in r raises the required return on both labor and capital. In order to increase the realized return on capital, for a given P_K, and keeping $\dot{P}_K$ equal to zero, L/K must increase. Therefore, the $\dot{P}_K= 0$ locus shifts downward and to the left in quadrant II, as shown in Figure 6. In order to increase the realized return on labor, keeping P_L constant, and

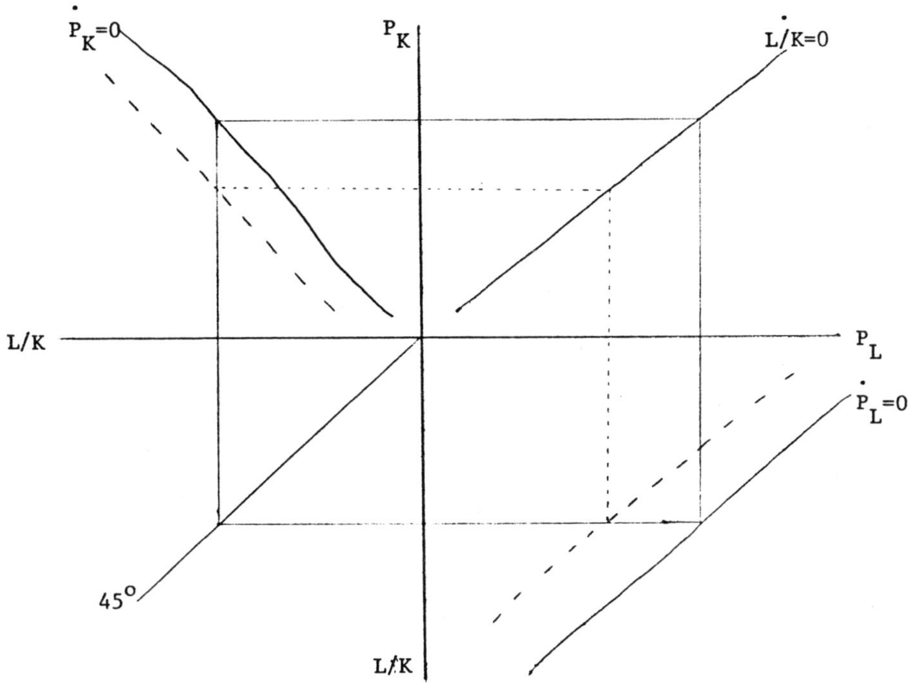

Figure 6

maintaining $\dot{P}_L = 0$, L/K must decrease. Therefore, the $\dot{P}_L = 0$ locus shifts upward and to the left in quadrant IV. Note that the $\dot{L/K} = 0$ locus is unaffected by the change in r. In igure 6, we observe that the steady state effects of an increase in r are to lower P_K and P_L. Hence, the rates of growth of capital and labor stocks are reduced in the long run. Essentially, P_K and P_L are reduced due to the greater discounting of future returns. The effect on steady state L/K is ambiguous.

Now consider an increase in the rate of physical depreciation of capital. The increase in δ increases the required rate of return on capital and hence shifts the $\dot{P}_K = 0$ locus downward and to the left, as explained above for an increase in r. The higher depreciation rate also requires a higher rate of gross investment to maintain a given net growth rate of the capital stock. Hence, the $\dot{L/K} = 0$ locus shifts upward in

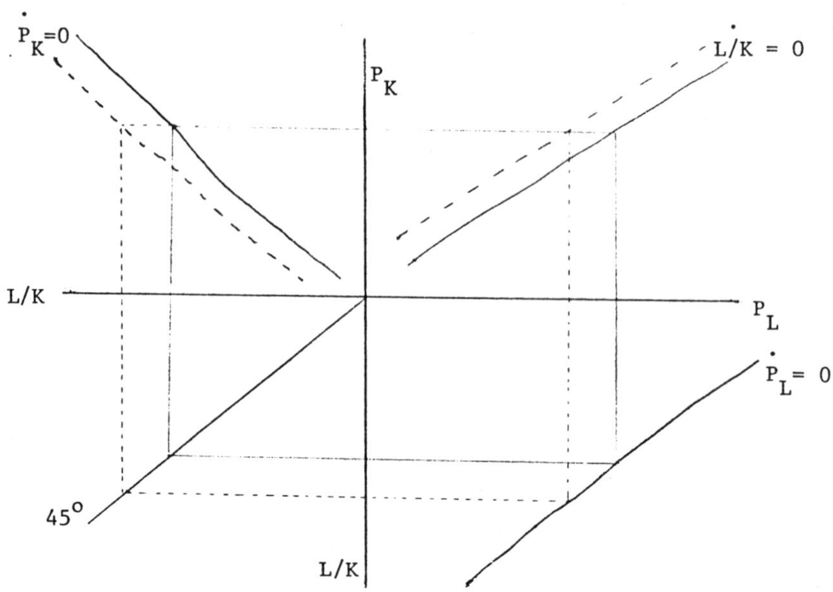

Figure 7

quadrant I. The increase in δ has no effect on the $\dot{P}_L = 0$ locus. In Figure 7, we observe that in the new steady state, L/K will be higher as there is substitution away from rapidly depreciating capital toward labor. The price of labor stock, P_L, decreases due to the lower marginal product of labor associated with the increased L/K. The effect on P_K is ambiguous. However, P_K must not rise by enough to increase the net growth rate of the capital stock. In the steady state, labor and capital grow at the same rate, and the decrease in P_L indicates a decrease in the net growth rate of labor and hence of capital.

The effects of an increase in μ, the depreciation rate of the labor stock, are symmetric to the effects of an increase in δ. The new steady state is characterized by a lower labor/capital ratio as there is substitution away from the rapidly depreciating labor stock toward capital. The lower labor/capital ratio reduces the rental accruing to installed capital and hence reduces P_K. The reduction in P_K decreases the steady state growth rate of capital. Therefore, the steady state growth rate of labor must decline also, although the effect on steady state P_L is ambiguous.

VI. Dynamics

The analysis of comparative steady states was greatly facilitated by the use of the four-quadrant diagram. We shall now use this diagram, along with an analysis of the roots of the system, to examine the dynamics of our system. The system consists of three differential equations which govern the motion of P_K, P_L, and L/K. Linearizing the system around the steady state, we obtain[1]

$$\text{(VI.1)}\quad \begin{bmatrix} \dot{P}_K \\ \dot{P}_L \\ \dot{L/K} \end{bmatrix} = \begin{bmatrix} r+\delta - I/K & 0 & \frac{-(1-\alpha)}{2a_o}P(\frac{L}{K})^{\alpha-1}A \\ 0 & r+\mu - I_L/L & \frac{1-\alpha}{2a_o}P(\frac{L}{K})^{\alpha-2}A \\ \frac{-L}{K}\frac{1}{c^{*\prime}(I/K)} & \frac{L}{K}\frac{1}{D^{*\prime}(I_L/L)} & 0 \end{bmatrix} \begin{bmatrix} P_K \\ P_L \\ L/K \end{bmatrix}$$

where all derivatives in the matrix are evaluated at the steady state. We can exploit the fact that the linearization is done around the steady state to simplify the system. In the steady state, $\dot{L/K} = 0$ which implies that $I/K - \delta = I_L/L - \mu$. Hence, $r+\delta - I/K$ equals $r+\mu - I_L/L$. We denote this common value x. For notational simplicity, let $G=((1-\alpha)/2a_o)P(L/K)^{\alpha-1} > 0$. Then the matrix of the system of differential equations may be written as

$$\text{(VI.2)}\quad \begin{bmatrix} x & 0 & -AG \\ 0 & x & (\frac{L}{K})^{-1}AG \\ -\frac{L}{K}\frac{1}{c^{*\prime}} & \frac{L}{K}\frac{1}{D^{*\prime}} & 0 \end{bmatrix}$$

---

[1]All of the entries in the matrix have been discussed earlier except for the zero in the lower right corner. This entry is equal to $\partial\dot{(L/K)}/\partial(L/K) = I_L/L - I/K - \mu + \delta$, which equals zero in the steady state.

The determinantal equation of this matrix is

$$\text{(VI.3)} \qquad -\lambda(x-\lambda)^2 - AG(L/K)(1/c*')(x-\lambda) - AG(1/D*')(x-\lambda) = 0,$$

which may be easily factored to

$$\text{(VI.4)} \qquad (x-\lambda)\{\lambda^2 - x\lambda - AG((L/K)(1/c*') + 1/D*')\} = 0.$$

Clearly, $\lambda=x$ is one root of this equation. From the quadratic formula, we find the other two roots of the system to be $\frac{x}{2} \pm \frac{1}{2}\sqrt{x^2+4AG(\frac{L}{K}\frac{1}{c*'} + \frac{1}{D*'})}$. The dynamic characteristics of the system depend on the sign of A. If A is negative, then all three roots have positive real parts and there is no path to the steady state equilibrium.[1] If A = 0, then the roots are x, x, and 0 so that there is no path to steady state equilibrium. If A is positive, then the system has two positive real roots and one negative real root. In this case, the steady state is a saddle point equilibrium with a unique path to steady state. Furthermore, since all three roots are real, there are no cycles in the path to steady state. To summarize, the only case in which there is a path to the steady state is the case in which A > 0. Recall that A > 0 is precisely the second order condition in the static maximization problem discussed in section II. Henceforth we shall assume that A > 0.

With the knowledge that there is a saddle point equilibrium and that there are no cycles in the movement toward the steady state, we can use the four-quadrant diagram to illustrate the path to the steady state. In Figure 8, we note six regions in P_K, L/K space. For each region, Table 1 indicates whether P_K is above or below its steady state value and its direction of movement. Also, the table indicates whether L/K is above or below its steady

---

[1] If $x^2+4AG((L/K)(1/c*')+(1/D*'))$ is positive, then all roots are positive and real. If $x^2+4AG((L/K)(1/c*')+(1/D*'))$ is negative, there is a complex conjugate pair of roots with positive real parts.

state value. Similarly, we note six regions in P_L, L/K space. In the accompanying table we note whether P_L is above or below its steady state value, its direction of movement, and whether L/K is above or below its steady state value.

Suppose that L/K is below its steady state value and that P_K and P_L are on the path to steady state. Inspection of table 1 indicates that P_K must be in region F and that P_L must be in region 2, so that P_K is low and rising, P_L is high and falling, and L/K is low and rising. Now suppose that L/K is above its steady state value and that P_K and P_L are on the path to steady state equilibrium. Inspection of the table indicates that P_K must be in region A and P_L must be in region 5, so that P_K is high and falling, P_L is low and rising and L/K is high and falling. The branches of the stable paths to the steady state are shown in Figure 8. At any point of time, L/K is given. The value of P_K is determined from the branch of the stable path in quadrant II and the value of P_L is determined from the branch

Table 1

Region	P_K	P_L	L/K
A	high, falling	-	high
B	high, rising	-	high
C	high, rising	-	low
D	low, falling	-	high
E	low, falling	-	low
F	low, rising	-	low
1	-	low, falling	low
2	-	high, falling	low
3	-	high, rising	low
4	-	low, falling	high
5	-	low, rising	high
6	-	high, rising	high

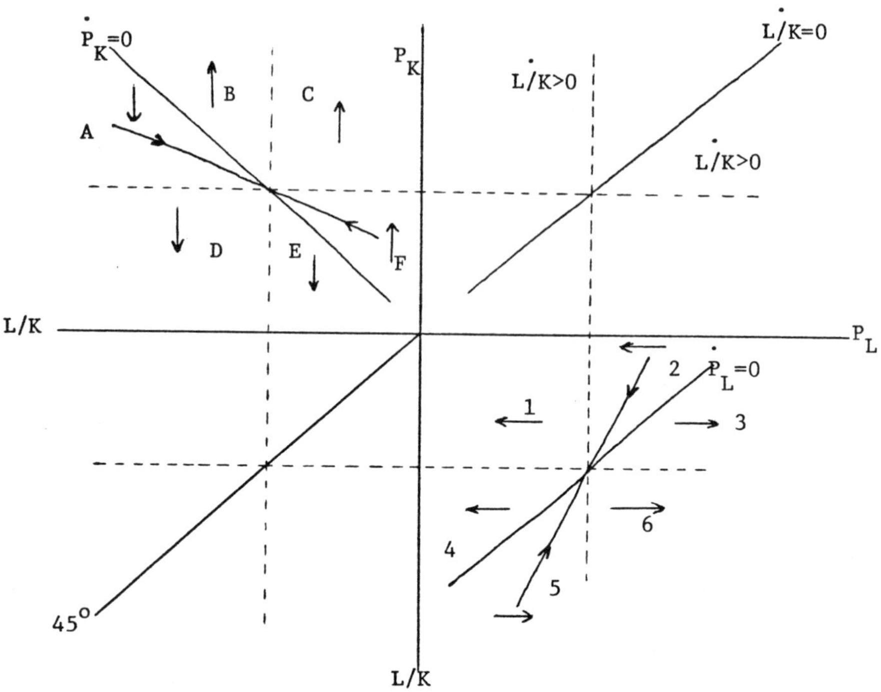

Figure 8

of the stable path in quadrant IV.[1]

VII. Dynamic Behavior of Capacity Utilization

We can now use the four-quadrant diagram, with the stable path to the steady state, to examine the behavior of capacity utilization. Recall that capacity utilization, β, is a decreasing function of L/K, given the value of P/w. Hence, capacity utilization moves inversely to L/K along the path to steady state. The conventional wisdom about capacity utilization and investment is that when capacity utilization is high, investment is high in order to ease the strain on capital. We can examine this proposition using the stable path to steady state equilibrium. Suppose

---

[1]If A were negative, the slopes of the $\dot{P}_L = 0$ locus and the $\dot{P}_K = 0$ locus would each have signs opposite to those in Figure 8. An exercise similar to that represented by Table 1 would fail to find any stable path to steady state equilibrium, as predicted from our analysis of the roots of the system.

that L/K is low relative to the steady state. Then, from figure 8, we observe that relative to the steady state, β is high, P_K is low and P_L is high. Each of these variables moves monotonically toward its steady state value. At first glance, these results appear to contradict the conventional wisdom since capacity utilization is high but P_K and investment in capital goods are low. However, we obtain these results because β represents labor stock utilization as well as capital stock utilization. In order to increase the rate of labor stock utilization, the firm must pay a higher wage bill. However, there are no increased costs associated with higher capital stock utilization _per se_. Thus, in this model, a high rate of resource utilization creates a greater incentive to expand the labor stock than to expand the capital stock. So when β is high, P_L is high but P_K is low, relative to the steady state.

We have shown that along the stable path to steady state, capacity utilization and investment in fixed capital are negatively related. However, this is not to deny the conventional wisdom. Suppose that there is an unanticipated increase in aggregate demand which is communicated to an individual firm as an increase in the price of output P. The increase in P increases the marginal revenue product of capital so that L/K must fall to keep P_K constant and to maintain $\dot{P}_K = 0$, since a fall in L/K reduces the marginal product of capital. The increase in P also increases the marginal revenue product of labor so that L/K must rise to maintain P_L constant and $\dot{P}_L$ equal to zero.[1] Suppose that the initial state of the system

[1]More formally, $\partial \dot{P}_K/\partial P = -(1-\alpha)(L/K)^{\alpha}(2\beta + a_1/2a_o) < 0$ so that L/K must fall for given P_K to maintain $\dot{P}_K$ equal to zero. Also $\partial \dot{P}_L/\partial P = -(A/2a_o)(L/K)^{\alpha-1} < 0$ so that L/K must rise, for given P_L, to maintain $\dot{P}_L$ equal to zero.

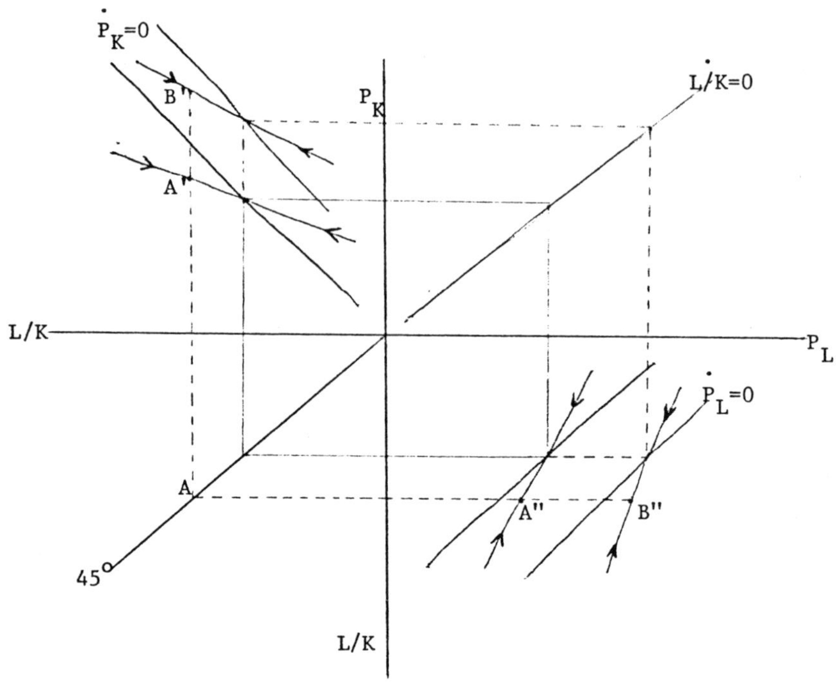

Figure 9

is represented by A, A', A". When the unanticipated jump in P occurs, the system jumps immediately to A, B', B". That is, there is an instantaneous jump in P_K, investment in capital goods, P_L, and investment in labor stock. Of course, L/K cannot jump instantaneously, but $\beta = (1/2a_o)(\frac{P}{w}(\frac{L}{K})^{\alpha-1} - a_1)$ jumps upward. Thus, in response to an unanticipated increase in output price, there is an immediate increase in capacity utilization and in the rates of investment in both quasi-fixed factors of production. This response is in accord with the conventional wisdom. Unanticipated changes in β, associated with unanticipated changes in demand, are positively associated with investment. Heuristically, the unanticipated increase in demand is met first by an increase in capacity utilization. The unanticipated increase in capacity utilization is a signal that the investment plans, for both capital and labor, must be revised upward.

VIII. Taxes

We now incorporate certain interesting features of the corporate tax environment into our analysis. Let τ be the rate of corporate taxation so that the after-tax operating profit of the firm is $(P\beta L^{\alpha}K^{1-\alpha} - w(a_o\beta^2+a_1\beta+a_2)L)(1-\tau)$. Let k be the rate of the investment tax credit. During the time interval dt, the gross cost of investment is $Ic(I/K)dt$. Hence, the cost of investment, net of the investment tax credit, is $(1-k)Ic(I/K)dt$. This net cost is used as the depreciation base of the newly installed capital.[1] If $J(x)$ is the amount of the depreciation base allowable as an expense for an asset of age x, then $\tau d = \int_0^\infty \tau J(x)e^{-rx}dx$ is the present value of the depreciation allowance for an asset with a depreciation base of unity.[2] Hence, the present value of the depreciation allowance on capital installed in time interval dt is $\tau d(1-k)Ic(I/K)dt$. Therefore, the net cost of investing at rate I during the interval dt is $(1-k)(1-\tau d)Ic(I/K)dt$. For notational simplicity, we define T to be equal to the relevant product of tax parameters, $(1-k)(1-\tau d)$.

The dynamic optimization problem of the firm is to maximize the present value of its stream of cash flow. The Hamiltonian for this problem is

$$\text{(VIII.1)}\quad H = \{(P\beta L^{\alpha}K^{1-\alpha}-w(a_o\beta^2+a_1\beta+a_2)L)(1-\tau) - TIc(I/K) - I_LD(I_L/L)\}\, e^{-rt} + P_Ke^{-rt}(I-\delta K) + P_Le^{-rt}(I_L-\mu L).$$

---

[1] Under the Long Amendment, the investment tax credit was subtracted from the cost of a capital good to determine the depreciation base. After the repeal of the Long Amendment, the investment tax credit was no longer subtracted to determine the depreciation base. Our formulas may be easily modified to account for this change.

[2] Note that r is an after-tax discount rate.

Differentiating H with respect to β and I_L and setting these partial derivatives equal to zero yields conditions identical to (III.4) and (III.7). To repeat these conditions, $2a_o\beta+a_1 = \frac{P}{W}(\frac{L}{K})^{\alpha-1}$ and $I_L/L = D*^{-1}(P_L)$. The corporate tax laws under consideration have no effect on either the current output decision or the relation between the price of labor and the rate of growth of the labor stock. Diffentiating H with respect to I and setting the derivative equal to zero yields $Tc*(I/K) = P_K$, which may be rewritten as

$$\text{(VIII.2)} \quad I/K = c*^{-1}(P_K/T).$$

This condition is easily interpreted as a version of Tobin's q. The investment capital ratio is an increasing function of the ratio of the value of capital in place to the tax-adjusted replacement cost of capital. We observe that an increase in the investment tax credit reduces T and hence tends to raise I/K, ceteris paribus. The same is true of a more generous depreciation allowance, which is represented formally by an increase in z.

The equations of motion of this system are derived exactly as in section IV. The equality of the required return and realized return on capital is given by

$$\text{(VIII.3)} \quad (r+\delta)P_K = (1-\tau)(1-\alpha)P\beta(\frac{L}{K})^{\alpha} + T(\frac{I}{K})^2c'(\frac{I}{K}) + \dot{P}_K .$$

Note that the first two components of the realized return are affected by the tax code. The realized return includes only the after-tax portion of the marginal revenue product of capital. As for the installation cost saving, the net purchase and installation costs must be adjusted downward to account for the investment tax credit and the depreciation allowance. We note that the $\dot{P}_K=0$ locus is still an upward sloping curve in P_K, L/K space.

The equality of realized and required rates of return on labor is expressed by

$$\text{(VIII.4)}\quad (r+\mu)P_L = (1-\tau)w((2\alpha-1)a_o\beta^2+(\alpha-1)a_1\beta - a_2) + (\frac{I_L}{L})^2 D'(\frac{I_L}{L}) + \dot{P}_L$$

The only effect of the tax code is to reduce the realized return on labor by including after-tax marginal revenue product of labor rather than the pre-tax marginal revenue product of labor. Hence, the $\dot{L/K} = 0$ locus is still a downward sloping locus in P_L, L/K space.

The tax code also affects the $\dot{L/K}=0$ locus since T, the tax-adjusted price of uninstalled capital has an effect on investment in capital goods. Consider a decrease in T which may arise from an increase in the rate of the investment tax credit or a liberalization of the depreciation allowance schedule. The decrease in T would raise capital goods investment, for a given P_K, since P_K/T rises. However, the equality of growth rates of labor and capital may be restored by a proportionate decrease in P_K, holding P_L constant. That is, the growth rates of capital and labor will remain equal to each other if P_K/T and P_L remain the same. Thus, the effect of a decrease in T is to shift the $\dot{L/K} = 0$ proportionately downward. Note that for a given T, this locus is still upward sloping in P_L, P_K space.

We have seen that the inclusion of certain features of the tax code into our analysis does not change the general characteristics of any of the loci $\dot{P}_K = 0$, $\dot{P}_L = 0$, or $\dot{L/K} = 0$. Therefore, the general features of the steady state solution are also unchanged by the inclusion of taxes. It is also true that the general characteristics of the dynamics of the system remain the same. Linearizing the system around its steady state, we obtain the following matrix for the system

$$\text{(VIII.5)}\quad \begin{bmatrix} x & 0 & -(1-\tau)GA \\ 0 & x & (1-\tau)GA(\frac{L}{K})^{-1} \\ -\frac{L}{K}\frac{1}{T}\frac{1}{c^{*\prime}} & \frac{L}{K}\frac{1}{D^{*\prime}} & 0 \end{bmatrix}$$

which is very similar to (VI.2). The roots of this matrix are x and $\frac{x}{2} \pm \frac{1}{2}\sqrt{x^2+4(1-\tau)GA((L/K)(1/Tc^{*\prime}) + (1/D^{*\prime}))}$ with the same interpretation as in Section VI. Since we have assumed that A is positive, the steady state is a saddle point equilibrium and the path to the steady state is monotonic.

The Investment Tax Credit

Suppose that there is an unanticipated permanent increase in the rate of the investment tax credit. As explained above, the increase in the investment tax credit reduces T and the $\dot{L/K} = 0$ locus shifts downward in proportion to T. The reduction in T also shifts the $\dot{P}_K = 0$ locus. The lower value for T increases the installation cost saving since $\frac{d}{dT}\left(T\left(\frac{I}{K}\right)^2 c'\left(\frac{I}{K}\right)\right) = -\frac{I}{K}\,c\left(\frac{I}{K}\right) < 0$. Therefore, in order to bring the realized return back down to the required return, for given P_K and holding $\dot{P}_K$ equal to zero, the labor/capital ratio must fall. Therefore, the decrease in T reduces L/K for given P_K while keeping $\dot{P}_K$ equal to 0 as shown in Figure 10.

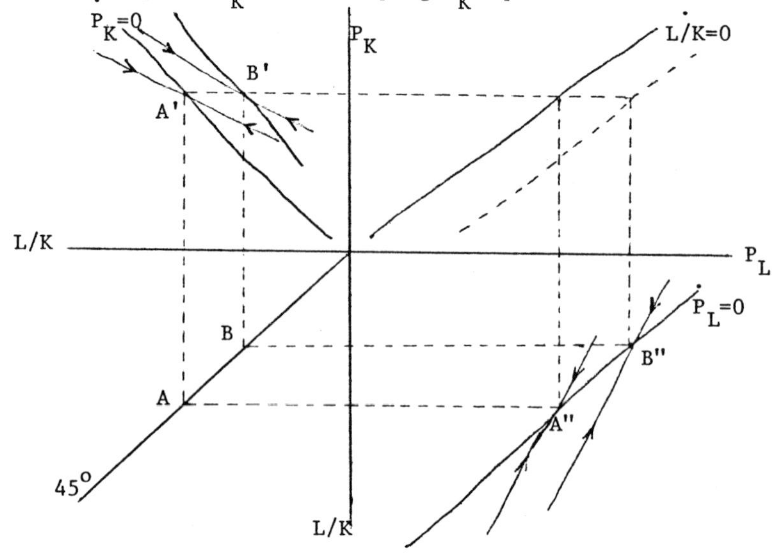

Figure 10

Under the original tax regime, the steady state is represented by A, A', A". After the permanent increase in the investment tax credit, the new steady state is represented by B, B', B" with a lower labor/capital ratio and a higher value for P_L. For comparative steady states, the investment tax credit leads to a shift from labor toward capital, as expected. The lower value of L/K increases the rentals accruing to the labor stock and hence increases P_L. The higher level of P_L raises the growth rate of the labor stock. Since labor and capital grow at the same rate in the steady state, the growth rate of capital must rise. Hence, P_K/T must increase although the effect on P_K is ambiguous.

Suppose that we are initially on the stable path to A, A', A" when the unanticipated investment tax credit goes into effect. The immediate effect is for P_K and P_L to jump to higher values. _A fortiori_, P_K/T jumps to a higher value. Hence the rates of investment in both stocks of resources jump upward immediately. Essentially, the reduction in T reduces the price of newly purchased uninstalled capital goods so that investment in capital goods will be increased in the present and over the future. The higher time path of the capital stock raises the marginal value product of labor so that the price of the labor stock rises, inducing a higher growth rate for this stock. After the initial jump in the rates of investment in both stocks, the investment rates move smoothly toward their steady state values.

IX. Concluding Remarks

In this paper, we have introduced limited ex post factor substitutability into a dynamic optimizing framework by treating labor as a quasi-fixed input and constraining the utilization rates of labor and capital to be equal. This model has provided a useful framework for examining optimal variations in capacity utilization and the relationship between investment and capacity utilization. We have shown that along the stable path to the steady state, capacity utilization and investment are inversely related, contrary to the conventional wisdom. However, in response to unanticipated demand shocks, capacity utilization and investment are positively associated. Essentially, the unanticipated strain on capacity causes the firm to revise its investment plan upward.

In order to achieve analytic tractability, this model has made two major simplifications. We have attempted to capture the essence of putty-clay by having no substitutability of labor for capital at any given point of time. However, the labor/capital ratio is allowed to change over time, even for existing units of capital. This substitutability of labor for capital on existing capital in place conflicts with the vintage capital model and strains the conventional interpretation of the putty-clay hypothesis. However, this simplification buys us a tractable model with reasonable results concerning limited ex post factor substitutability. The second major simplification is that the utilization rates of labor and capital are always equal. This assumption could be relaxed in a variety of ways. However, as long as the two utilization rates are positively related at each point of time, it seems that the basic results of this model would still hold. By constraining the two utilization rates to be equal, we reduce the number of decision variables and obtain a system which can be solved graphically. Aside from the exploration of the effects of these two simplifications,there are other dimensions along which this model could be extended. The effect of uncertainty, either demand uncertainty or uncertainty about future tax laws, would be an interesting extension of the model. As for empirical extensions of the model, there remains a range of questions about the proper specification and estimation of an investment equation based on the value of installed capital relative to reproduction cost. Some of these issues have been discussed in Essay II, and it seems that the same estimation technique is applicable to the investment equation of this essay. However, in addition to an investment equation for fixed capital, there is a related equation for investment in the labor stock. Each of these investment equations depends on expectations about future rentals to labor and to capital. To the extent that the future rentals on labor and capital are interrelated, the expectational errors in the two equations are correlated. This correlation might be exploited to improve the efficiency of estimation.

BIBLIOGRAPHY

Abel, Andrew B., "Expectational Error and Coefficient Bias in a Distributed Lead Equation," September 15, 1977. Unpublished.

Ando, Albert K., Franco Modigliani, Robert Rasche, and Steven J. Turnovsky, "On the Role of Expectations of Price and Technological Change in an Investment Function," International Economic Review, 15 (June 1974), pp. 384-414.

Arrow, Kenneth J., "Optimal Capital Policy With Irreversible Investment," Value, Capital and Growth, Essays in Honor of Sir John Hicks, James N. Wolfe (ed.) (Edinburgh: Edinburgh University Press, 1968), pp. 1-19.

Bischoff, Charles W., "Hypothesis Testing and the Demand for Capital Goods," Review of Economics and Statistics, 51 (August 1969), pp. 354-68.

________, "Business Investment in the 1970's: A Comparison of Models," Brookings Papers on Economic Activity 1, (1971), pp. 13-58.

Brainard, William C. and James Tobin, "Pitfalls in Financial Model Building," American Economic Review Papers and Proceedings, 58 (May 1968), pp. 99-122.

Ciccolo, John H., Jr., "Four Essays on Monetary Policy," unpublished Doctoral dissertation, Yale University, May 1975.

Coen, Robert M., "Tax Policy and Investment Behavior: Comment," American Economic Review, 59 (June 1969), pp. 370-79.

Economic Report of the President (Washington, D.C.: United States Government Printing Office, 1977).

Eisner, Robert, "Tax Policy and Investment Behavior: Comment," American Economic Review (June 1969), pp. 379-88.

________ and M. I. Nadiri, "Investment Behavior and Neoclassical Theory," Review of Economics and Statistics, 50 (August 1968), pp. 369-82.

________, "Neoclassical Theory of Investment Behavior: A Comment," Review of Economics and Statistics, 52 (May 1970), pp. 216-22.

________ and R. H. Strotz, "Determinants of Business Investment," in Commission on Money and Credit Impacts of Monetary Policy (Englewood Cliffs, N.J.: Prentice-Hall, 1963), pp. 59-337.

Engle, Robert F. and Duncan K. Foley, "An Asset Price Model of Aggregate Investment," International Economic Review, 16 (October 1975), pp. 625-47.

Faurot, David J., "Interrelated Demand for Capital and Labor in a Globally Optimal Flexible Accelerator Model," Review of Economics and Statistics, 60 (February 1978), pp. 25-32

Feldstein, Martin S. and Michael Rothschild, "Towards an Economic Theory of Replacement Investment," Econometrica, 42 (May 1974), pp. 393-423.

Flavin, Marjorie, "The Adjustment of Consumption to Changing Expectations about Future Income," September 20, 1977, unpublished.

Foley, Duncan and Miguel Sidrauski, "Portfolio Choice, Investment and Growth," American Economic Review, 60 (March 1970), pp. 44-63.

Fuss, Melvyn A., "The Structure of Technology Over Time: A Model for Testing the 'Putty-Clay' Hypothesis," Econometrica, 45 (November 1977), pp. 1797-1821.

Gould, John P., "Adjustment Costs in the Theory of the Firm," Review of Economic Studies, 35 (January 1968), pp. 47-55.

Hall, Robert E., "The Dynamic Effects of Fiscal Policy in an Economy With Foresight," Review of Economic Studies, 38 (April 1971), pp. 229-44.

________, "Investment, Interest Rates and the Effects of Stabilization Policies," Brookings Papers on Economic Activity (1977), pp. 61-121.

________ and Dale W. Jorgenson, "Tax Policy and Investment Behavior," American Economic Review, 57 (June 1967), pp. 391-414.

________, "Tax Policy and Investment Behavior: Reply and Further Results," American Economic Review, 59 (June 1969), pp. 388-401.

________, "Application of the Theory of Optimal Capital Accumulation," in Tax Incentives and Capital Spending, Gary Fromm (ed.), Studies of Government Finance, The Brookings Institution, Washington, D.C. (1971), p. 9-60.

Jorgenson, Dale W., "Capital Theory and Investment Behavior," American Economic Review Papers and Proceedings, 53 (May 1963), pp. 247-59.

________ and James A. Stephenson, "Issues in the Development of the Neoclassical Theory of Investment Behavior," Review of Economics and Statistics, 51 (August 1969), pp. 346-53.

Keynes, John Maynard, The General Theory of Employment, Interest and Money (London: Macmillan, 1936).

Krugman, Paul, "A Simplified Theory of Investment," February 1977, unpublished.

Lucas, Robert E. Jr., "Optimal Investment Policy and the Flexible Accelerator," International Economic Review, 8 (February 1967), pp. 78-85.

________, "Adjustment Costs and the Theory of Supply," Journal of Political Economy, 75 (August 1967), pp. 321-34.

Mussa, Michael, "Market Value and the Investment Decision in an Adjustment Cost Model of Firm Behavior," Department of Economics, University of Rochester Discussion Paper 74-15, July 1974.

________, "External and Internal Adjustment Costs and the Theory of Aggregate and Firm Investment," Economica, 44 (May 1977), pp. 163-78.

Muth, John F., "Rational Expectations and the Theory of Price Movements," Econometrica (July 1961).

Nadiri, M. Ishaq and Sherwin Rosen, "Interrelated Factor Demand Functions," American Economic Review, 59 (September 1969), pp. 457-71.

Rothschild, Michael, "On the Cost of Adjustment," Quarterly Journal of Economics, 85 (November 1971), pp. 605-22.

Samuelson, Paul A., "Tax Deductibility of Economic Depreciation to Insure Invariant Valuations," Journal of Political Economy, 72 (December 1964), pp. 604-6.

Söderstrom, Hans Tson, "Production and Investment Under Costs of Adjustment, A Survey," Zeitschrift für Nationalökomie, 36 (1976), pp. 369-88.

Tobin, James, "Money, Capital and Other Stores of Value," American Economic Review Papers and Proceedings, 51 (May 1961), pp. 26-37.

________, "A General Equilibrium Approach to Monetary Theory," Journal of Money, Credit and Banking, 1 (February 1969), pp. 15-29.

Treadway, Arthur B., "On Rational Entrepreneurial Behavior and the Demand for Investment," Review of Economic Studies, 36 (1969) pp. 227-39.

________, "The Globally Optimal Flexible Accelerator," Journal of Economic Theory, 7 (1974), pp. 17-39.

Witte, James G., Jr., "The Microfoundations of the Social Investment Function," Journal of Political Economy, 71 (October 1963), pp. 441-56.